Literacy Strategies

Strategies

for Grades 4-12

Reinforcing the
Threads of Reading

Karen Tankersley

ASCD

Alexandria, Virginia USA

ASCD®

1703 N. Beauregard St., Alexandria, VA 22311-1714 USA
Phone: 800-933-2723 or 703-578-9600 Fax: 703-575-5400
Web site: www.ascd.org E-mail: member@ascd.org
Author guidelines: www.ascd.org/write

Gene R. Carter, *Executive Director;* Nancy Modrak, *Director of Publishing;* Julie Houtz, *Director of Book Editing & Production;* Ernesto Yermoli, *Project Manager;* Reece Quiñones, *Senior Graphic Designer;* Jim Beals, *Typesetter;* Dina Murray Seamon, *Production Specialist*

All Web links in this book are correct as of the publication date below but may have become inactive or otherwise modified since that time. If you notice a deactivated or changed link, please e-mail books@ascd.org with the words "Link Update" in the subject line. In your message, please specify the Web link, the book title, and the page number on which the link appears.

ISBN-13: 978-1-4166-2434-9

Paperback ISBN: 1-4166-0154-6 ASCD product #104428   s6/05

e-books: retail PDF ISBN: 1-4166-0259-3 netLibrary ISBN: 1-4166-0257-7 ebrary ISBN: 1-4166-0258-5

Also available as an e-book through ebrary, netLibrary, and many online booksellers (see Books in Print for the ISBNs).

Quantity discounts for the paperback book: 10–49 copies, 10%; 50+ copies, 15%; for 500 or more copies, call 800-933-2723, ext. 5634, or 703-575-5634.

Library of Congress Cataloging-in-Publication Data

Tankersley, Karen, 1952-
    Literacy strategies for grades 4-12 : reinforcing the threads of reading / Karen Tankersley.
        p. cm.
    Includes bibliographical references.
    ISBN 1-4166-0154-6 (alk. paper)
    1. Reading (Elementary)—United States. 2. Reading (Secondary)—United States. 3. Literacy—Study and teaching (Elementary)—United States. 4. Literacy—Study and teaching (Secondary)—United States. I. Association for Supervision and Curriculum Development. II. Title.

    LB1573.T26 2005
    428.4'071—dc22

                                        2005009482

17 16 15 14   7 8 9 10 11 12

This book is dedicated to

my husband, Fred.

Thank you for being the wind

beneath my wings.

Literacy Strategies
for Grades 4-12

Reinforcing the Threads of Reading

Introduction

Teaching is not simply the ability to create a fantastic lesson plan for one day: rather, it is the ability to weave various experiences together to form a tapestry that provides the opportunities for children to immerse themselves in quality literature and develop as sophisticated readers.
                              —Frank Serafini (2001, p. xvi)

Over the past decade, researchers and policymakers in the United States have focused on preventing reading difficulties in the early grades. Under the reauthorization of the U.S. Elementary and Secondary Education Act in 2001, the federal government pledged $900 million to the states for professional development and the implementation of "research-proven" reading practices at the preK–3rd grade level. Although there is no dispute that early reading success is essential, too little has been done to address the needs of students and teachers beyond the 3rd grade.

A solid foundation in phonemic awareness, vocabulary, and general background knowledge is essential for young students if they are to become successful readers. Research clearly shows that students who fall behind their classmates as early as 1st grade will fall further behind as time passes (Francis, Shaywitz, Steubing, Shaywitz, & Fletcher, 1996; Good, Simmons, & Smith, 1998; Torgensen & Burgess, 1998). According to Juel (1988), 87 percent of children who were poor readers at the end of 1st grade were still poor readers by the end of 4th grade— and 75 percent of those who underperformed in 3rd grade were still behind in high school, often by as much as four years (National Center for Education Statistics, 2003). Stanovich (1986) refers to this phenomenon as the "Matthew Effect" (after the New Testament verse Matthew 25:29, source of the adage, "the rich get richer and the poor get poorer"): over time, those who do well from the start tend to improve, while those who begin poorly tend to do worse. Because the No Child Left Behind (NCLB) legislation provides nasty consequences for lack of "adequate yearly progress" in core content areas, educators across the United States have been scrambling to find ways to address these literacy gaps.

The International Center for Leadership in Education reports that entry-level jobs in the United States now have higher reading requirements than are necessary to graduate from high school (Daggett, 2004). Because more and more jobs are being outsourced overseas, U.S. students cannot afford to be caught unprepared to compete in the global workforce. The literacy demands that young workers will face in the 21st-century workplace will far exceed anything that has been required of past generations (Moore, Bean, Birdyshaw, & Rycik, 1999). According to Snow (2002):

> An employment market with few blue-collar jobs but many service-related and information-based jobs is increasingly demanding high school graduation—the minimum essential for employment. Moreover, advanced vocational or academic training is a requirement now for a wide variety of positions that previously might have gone to high school dropouts. Thus, ensuring advanced literacy achievement for all students is no longer a luxury but an economic necessity. (p. 4)

Whether we like it or not, demands for high literacy levels in the workforce are driving the national thinking behind NCLB, which demands that all schools progress toward ensuring student proficiency in the major content areas by 2013–2014. Though many are still far from meeting that mark, U.S. students at the lower grades are demonstrating solid progress in literacy: According to the National Center for Education Statistics (2001), the United States ranks second only to Finland in international comparisons of 4th grade reading performance. By 8th grade, however, the reading performance of U.S. students falls to the middle of the pack—behind Finland, France, Sweden, New Zealand, Hungary, Iceland, and Switzerland (Allington, 2001).

U.S. critics cite the lack of student improvement on the National Assessment of Educational Progress (NAEP) test over the past decade as evidence of a "crisis" in education. The NAEP (National Center for Education Statistics, 2003) shows that even in 4th grade, where overall student performance is better than in the earlier grades, fully 37 percent of U.S. students failed to meet the most basic reading performance level. By 8th grade, only 32 percent of students scored at or above the proficiency level, and 26 percent failed to qualify for the basic reading proficiency.

As students get older, NAEP scores continue to show significant decline. The NAEP results for 2002 show 12th grade reading scores lower than those in 1992 and 1998. According to NAEP (National Center for Education Statistics, 2002) results, only 36 percent of the nation's 12th grade students were proficient readers, and 26 percent were sent into the labor market without adequate preparation in even the most basic of reading skills. It should be noted that these dismal statistics are only for students who remained in the school system during their senior year; many of the most struggling students will have dropped out long before. This means that the number of students who are not succeeding at literacy upon graduation is even greater than the NAEP results show. How can these students be expected to compete in a labor market that demands higher levels of education and skill?

The social and economic consequences of leaving school without basic reading skills are profound, ranging from failure to graduate to unemployment. Without an adequate education, young people may have trouble managing their finances and family lives. Criminal records indicate that at least half of all teenagers and young adults with criminal histories, and half of those with substance abuse problems, have reading difficulties; some states even predict their future need for prisons based on their 4th grade reading failure rates (Lyon, 2001).

When we look closely at the data, there are stark contrasts among students. Males at all grade levels consistently have lower reading rates than females, and students of black, Hispanic, and Native American descent scored below their Caucasian and Asian counterparts by wide margins (National Center for Education Statistics, 2002, 2003). These glaring gaps in performance suggest a strong need to increase teacher training and improve the teaching of literacy skills in all middle and high schools. One way to do this is to strive for what Langer refers to as "high literacy" (Bereiter & Scardamalia, 1987; Langer, 1999); She defines this as "a 'well-developed' curriculum that teaches students to 'read' the social meanings, the rules and structures, and the linguistic and cognitive routines to make things work in the real world of English language use, and that knowledge becomes available as options when students confront new situations" (Langer, 1999, p. 1). Clearly, high literacy can help students to be independent, thorough thinkers ready for the workplace of tomorrow.

Reading Is Linear, Not Holistic

Over the years, I have come to believe that reading is not a holistic process that "just happens," but rather a linear one that builds hierarchically, as does development in math. A huge factor in literacy is learning to make connections between what we already know and the new information we are learning. Reading is about understanding and being able to process what we see at the metacognitive level; without comprehension, true reading does not occur.

Reading growth does not end at a specific age; we never truly master reading, but continue to build our skills and background knowledge over our lifetimes. All readers continually cycle back through different levels of understanding as they read (see Figure I.1).

Figure I.1
Hierarchy of Reading Threads

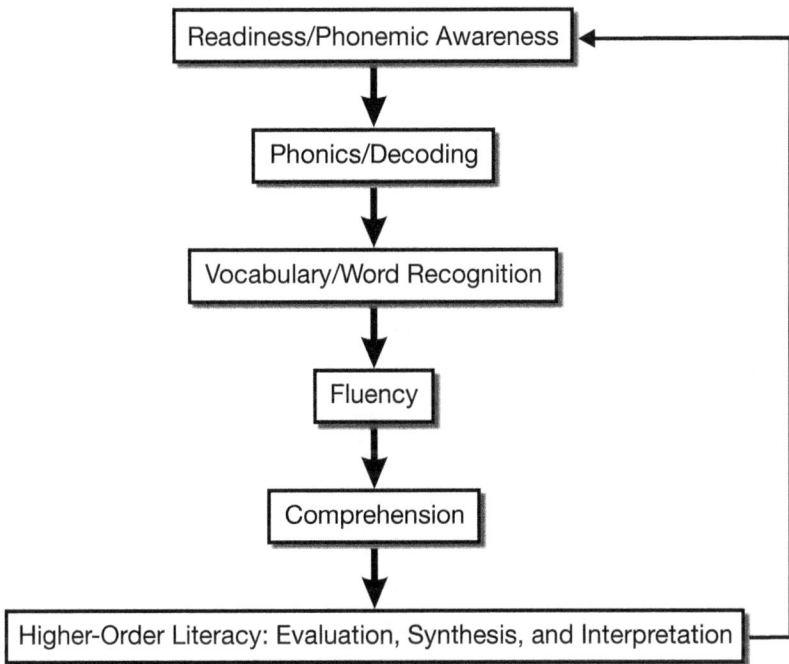

Unfortunately, reading difficulties often start before students even enter school: Researchers have identified vocabulary gaps in children as young as three that could prevent them from doing well later in life (Hart & Risley, 2003). According to Snow, Burns, and Griffin (1998), children who do not develop strong decoding skills by the end of 1st grade may well become struggling readers throughout their lives.

To become good readers, children should be talked and read to extensively and taught the concepts of letters, words, rhyme, and patterns. After seeing the same "cat, sat, rat" patterns over and over again in nursery rhymes, songs, and stories, children should be able to recognize other types of patterns. These readers have developed the foundational skill of "phonemic awareness"—the first thread of the reading tapestry. Once they understand that spoken and written words are related, the next step is to learn that some words are not easily identifiable by a predictable pattern and must be identified by their sequence of letters. This is how children develop phonics and decoding skills.

When I mention that phonics is a key thread of reading, some people argue that they learned using the "look-see" method or the "Dick and Jane" whole-word approach and can read just fine. I learned to read with "Dick and Jane" books too, but I was also read to a lot as a child. Because of this, I came to school with a solid background in the patterns of nursery rhymes and a sense of print from years of being read to on my mother's lap. I can even remember my teachers showing the class how "book" and "look" had similar endings as we learned to read each new vocabulary word. The authors of the "Dick and Jane" books deliberately limited the vocabulary to no more than 300 words in each reader, which helps students memorize visual patterns more quickly. Still, there is documented evidence that the "Dick and Jane" readers are not always successful with children who do not start school with a solid background in phonemic awareness (Kismaric & Heiferman, 1996).

Once students have learned to decode written words, they are ready to start developing fluency skills, which are directly tied to vocabulary knowledge. As vocabulary and background knowledge in the content increases, so does fluency—and when reading flows easily, comprehension increases. When the reader has limited background knowledge, comprehension remains limited. The more knowledge the reader gains, the more processing power he or she can devote to deeper levels of understanding. Eventually, the reader will have sufficient background knowledge to analyze and evaluate the material being read; it is at this point that the reader is truly interacting with the text and using metacognition to monitor his or her reading. Until students can truly understand the text they are reading, they cannot become problem solvers or critical thinkers with regards to the material.

Content Reading Patterns

In content instruction, each discipline has unique features and predictable organizational patterns that suggest specific ways of approaching text. As experts in their chosen disciplines, teachers have mastered these patterns and want to share their content knowledge with students.

For years, teachers have blamed textbooks for their students' learning difficulties. Over and over again, I have heard teachers say that if their students could actually *read* their textbooks, then their performance would improve. We balk at being told that we must now teach reading on top of teaching math, science, or social studies. We remind our administrators that we have been trained as specialists in our discipline, not as reading instructors. Yet there are many ways that we can help our students to improve their reading comprehension (see Chapter 4).

Unfortunately, too few teachers have been trained in how to help students develop reading skills in a specific content area. As Ruddell (2001) notes, "To think deeply in any subject area, students must learn the language of that subject area and be able to read and write fluently in that language; therefore, it is the subject area specialist (the classroom teacher)—not the reading teacher down the hall—who is responsible for teaching those skills" (p. 16). Eisner (1998) reminds us that assessment measures should reflect the tasks that students will encounter in the real world, as opposed to examples developed specifically for school. Instead of just having students answer questions at the end of every textbook chapter, educators should give students meaningful work to do—and introduce them to the thinking skills required for that discipline.

This book shows how teachers can use their content expertise to help students link their background knowledge to a given discipline, and in the process become strategic, thoughtful, high-level thinkers who are prepared to join the workforce. As the chapters that follow illustrate, true reading proficiency is the product of distinct and equally integral threads, all woven together to create the larger whole.

The Struggling Reader

The Brain and Reading

Wolfe and Nevills (2004) describe the brain as a hierarchy of low-level decoding skills and high-level comprehension-making skills. They write that at "the higher levels are the neural systems that process semantics (the meaning of language), syntax (organizing words into comprehensible sentences), and discourse (writing and speaking). Underlying these abilities are the lower-level phonological skills (decoding) dedicated to deciphering the reading code" (p. 26). All of these systems must function well in order for individuals to read quickly and make meaning from the text.

Dyslexia and Poor Readers

Dyslexia is a reading disability that can affect those who otherwise demonstrate the intelligence, motivation, and education to develop into good readers (Lyon, Shaywitz, & Shaywitz, 2003). It affects 80 percent of people identified as "learning disabled," and is believed to affect an estimated 5 to 17 percent of Americans (Shaywitz, 2003). Dyslexia is genetic: 25 to 50 percent of those with a dyslexic parent also have the disorder (Scarborough, 1984). According to Shaywitz (2003), dyslexia affects boys and girls equally, but boys tend to be identified more frequently as having the disorder due to their more disruptive behavior in the classroom. However, this conclusion has recently been disputed by the research of Dr. Michael Rutter at King's College in London, which found dyslexia to be present in 18 to 22 percent of boys and only 8 to 13 percent of girls (Tanner, 2004).

As a result of new technology, neuroscientists are learning more and more about how the brain operates and what causes dyslexia. Because reading is a complex brain activity, a lot can go wrong as children develop into readers. Each potential problem area must be examined when reading difficulties occur so that the right solutions can be provided. Because reading begins with visual input, any vision problems can inhibit the ability to process print effectively. Some poor readers may have subtle sensory deficits in visual processing, such as poor visual acuity or slower-than-normal eye movements (Berninger, 2002). In addition, any type of hearing impairment, such as chronic ear infections during the preschool years, can harm the language development of young children. Those who cannot process sound quickly enough can have trouble distinguishing similar consonant sounds (such as *p* or *b*). Training in sound-symbol correspondence and aural acuity will help these children improve their ability to process the sounds they hear and read.

A deficit in the language systems of the brain seems to be the problem that most frequently affects struggling readers. There are three main areas in the brain devoted to reading:

■ The inferior frontal gyrus, or Broca's area, situated at the front of the brain and responsible for articulating speech;

■ The parieto-temporal area, situated at the back of the brain and responsible for analyzing and sounding out parts of words; and

■ The occipito-temporal area, also situated at the back of the brain and responsible for synthesizing all information related to words and sound, and thus for recognizing words instantly.

According to Shaywitz and Shaywitz (2004), functional magnetic resonance imaging (fMRI) reveals striking differences in the ways that dyslexic and nondyslexic readers process what they read: Whereas nondyslexic readers experience activity in the left Broca's area and the left parieto-temporal and occipito-temporal areas of the brain, dyslexic readers display over-activity in the frontal area, but very little activity in the left rear areas of the brain that nondyslexic readers use. These findings suggest that the brains of dyslexic readers try to compensate for an inability to use the left rear parieto-temporal and occipito-temporal areas by over-activating Broca's area on both sides of the brain.

Although the dyslexic readers often learn to read, the task was slow and laborious, and the patterns of over-reliance on the inferior frontal gyrus continued into adulthood. Exciting new research is now changing the long-held belief that a child with dyslexia is destined to become a dyslexic adult.

In a study by Shaywitz et al. (2003), researchers provided 2nd and 3rd grade struggling readers with 50 minutes of daily individual tutoring on how letters and letter combinations represent the sounds of speech. This explicit tutoring, provided by specially trained, certified teachers, was given in addition to regular classroom reading instruction. After eight months (105 hours), the students in the study demonstrated significant gains in reading fluency. Scans of their brains showed new activity in the left rear parieto-temporal and occipito-temporal areas that had not been present prior to the tutoring. One year following the study, the students were reading accurately and fluently without any additional tutoring, and fMRI scans revealed that all three left-sided areas of their brains were now much more activated as in a normal reader. A control group that had received nonphonological reading instruction did not show reading improvement or changes in brain function. This exciting study shows that dyslexia may be affected through appropriate instruction at an early age.

The Gap Between Good and Poor Readers

The National Center for Education Statistics (NCES) found that children who are read to three or more times per week are more likely to know their letters, count to 20 or higher, write their own names, and actually read when they enter school (Nord, Lennon, Liu, & Chandler, 1999). The center also found that white children were read to more often than black or Latino children (NCES, 2003). According to Yarosz and Barnett (2001), the educational level of students' mothers and the wealth of their families were among the factors most strongly associated with reading frequency: 74 percent of children living in poverty were read to by family members before entering kindergarten, as compared to 87 percent of more affluent children.

Juel (1988) reports that by the end of 1st grade, students proficient at reading will have seen an average of 18,681 words of running text, whereas those who are struggling will have only seen 9,975. It is no wonder that, given half as much practice as their more proficient peers, struggling readers lost ground in decoding, automaticity, fluency, and vocabulary growth. The problem was not that the children were not developing skills— they were—but rather that they had fallen behind their classmates and were never able to catch up. By high school, many of these students will have fallen behind their peers by as much as four years (Shaywitz, 2003).

Sometimes students who make adequate progress in the early grades begin to struggle again around the beginning of 4th grade—what teachers refer to as "the 4th grade slump." Chall, Jacobs, and Baldwin (1990) identified a drop in the reading scores of students between the 3rd and 4th grades, particularly those with low incomes. The researchers suggest that reasons for this could include the appearance of fewer picture clues in 4th grade texts, the abundance of new vocabulary words, and an expectation that students absorb information from the text rather than simply read for plot. They also point out that around the 4th grade, teachers shift their focus from "learning to read" to "reading to learn" in the different content areas. However, Hirsch (2003) disagrees that the gap widens in the 4th grade. He suggests that "reading tests make the comprehension gap *seem* much greater in fourth grade because the texts used in earlier grades are heavily focused on testing early reading skills (like decoding) and do not try to measure the full extent of the vocabulary differences between the groups" (p. 10).

It is certainly no surprise, given their years of frustration, that struggling readers typically are anxious about school. They tend not to be very motivated, and often lack self-confidence regarding their ability to read (Kos, 1991). Struggling readers often attribute their problems to the difficulty of the task, interference, too much noise, vision problems, or unfair teachers; seldom do they acknowledge that their own lack of skill is at the heart of the issue. Many give up trying to improve altogether, believing that it is hopeless for them. In turn, teachers attribute the reluctance of these students to participate in activities as either defiance or lack of motivation, and do not know how to address the problem.

Older struggling readers, who have experienced many years of frustration and failure, are often skilled evaders who try to either "hide out or act out" so they can avoid reading in front of their peers. Cope (1997) notes that unrehearsed oral reading was the *single* most negative experience reported by adolescents about their entire school experience.

Researcher Mary Ellen Vogt (1989, 2000) examined how students perceived as either high or low achievers by their teachers were treated in class and came to some startling conclusions. In classrooms where students were perceived as high performers, Vogt found that teachers

- Talked less and encouraged more interactions among students,
- Allowed for more creative and generative approaches to learning,
- Offered opportunities for independent work,
- Had warmer and more personal relationships with students, and
- Spent little time on behavior or classroom management issues.

On the other hand, teachers working with perceived low performers

- Prepared more structured lessons,
- Allowed fewer opportunities for student creativity,
- Covered less content,
- Rewarded students for "trying hard" rather than for "good thinking,"
- Spent a significant amount of time on behavior and management issues, and
- Had less congenial relationships with students due to their heavy emphasis on discipline.

Little wonder that struggling students find school less than an encouraging place to spend their time.

While many low-performing students shun outside reading, not all of them do. Some read music, sports, or pop culture magazines regularly. They spend hours researching their favorite pop or rap singers on the Internet, and frequently spend many hours reading online. Clearly, young people can motivate themselves to read what interests them. For this reason, our classrooms must become inviting places that make students want to partake of what we offer. Reading must be seen as helpful, interesting, and a means to achieve the big-picture goals in their lives.

Motivating Struggling Readers

Motivation is strongly affected by two variables: whether we expect to be successful at a task, and how much value we place on that success (Wigfield & Asher, 1984). People generally believe they are successful because of one of three reasons: ability, effort, or luck. Highly successful people tend to believe that they succeed because of ability and fail due to lack of effort (Marzano, Pickering, & Pollock, 2001). Poorly motivated people, on the other hand, tend to attribute success to luck and failure to a lack of ability instead of lack of effort (Weiner, 1979). After many encounters with failure, some individuals may begin to believe that they are not capable of success, and give up without even trying. Teachers must continually reinforce the connection between effort and achievement with struggling students. An environment where success is possible and students set reachable goals can have a profound, positive effect on struggling students (Marzano, Pickering, & Pollock, 2001).

Unfortunately, we often have to present content to our students that is outside their realm of interest or prior experience. It has been demonstrated time and again that when we are interested in a subject, we are better prepared to relate to the information being presented to us. Rasinski (2003) calls this the "Michael Jordan effect." To get where he wanted to be professionally, Michael Jordan had to undergo many long hours of tedious practice to become an expert in his sport, and was self-motivated to do so. The task for teachers, then, is not selecting work that is particularly exciting, but rather work that is meaningful and helps students to be self-motivated.

Students have to know what's in it for them before their interest can be maximized.

If we want struggling readers to improve, we have to help them see reading as a bridge to learning more about the things that matter to them. For example, one fun way to introduce students to the concepts of grammar is the book *Idioms for Aliens: A Grammar Revue of Plays and Verse* by Ed Butts (2004), which helps students to learn about grammar while participating in a Reader's Theater or choral reading experience. The verse is fun, and makes learning seem almost incidental.

Another idea is to have students write diary entries based on biographical information about a historical figure they have studied. The entries should include not only historical facts, but also the characters' thoughts and feelings about the events of their time.

Because most students today are computer literate, yet another option is to have them develop Web sites on the topic they are studying. Have students view examples, consider the type of information they'd like to share with visiting guests, and provide links to relevant sites. Many districts now provide space for student-developed projects on their servers; for those that do not, many free Web hosting services are available.

Taking Away Excuses

Word-by-word readers often concentrate so hard on decoding that they do not absorb the meaning of what they read. These students must be reminded that when this happens, they have to stop and use a fix-up strategy such as rereading, considering the context, or asking for clarification. Many struggling readers simply quit when the going gets tough. We must help them learn that all readers have lapses in understanding, and that the difference between good readers and poor ones lies in what they do when comprehension breaks down.

Struggling readers must be exposed to a wide variety of text genres and types, including newspaper and magazine articles, novels, and Web sites. Understanding the features specific to different genres and types of text allows students to better predict what comes next and how the text will be presented. Conducting read-alouds and walking students through thinking aloud about what they read can also be of help.

Many struggling readers are unfamiliar with everyday terms that the rest of us take for granted—terms such as *compare*, *contrast*, *infer*, and *discuss*. For these students, we must provide specific modeled lessons coupled with guided feedback on their performance. For example, we must help them learn how to compare two concepts, or to summarize a text and see how it connects to events in their own world. We must take away students' excuses for not understanding what they read by providing the guidance and solid skills to overcome their difficulties.

Motivational Strategies for Struggling Readers

Varied Texts

When the current school system was conceived back in the late 1800s, schoolchildren were being shaped for life in the Industrial Age. Workers were needed who could sit at assembly lines and complete their tasks in isolation, without interacting with others. For this reason, schools were organized around independent work, and competition among students was seen as productive. But times have changed, and we need to bring our instructional practices into line with the skills necessary for success in today's society. Nowadays, employers want people who can be good team players, working collaboratively rather than in isolation. Even educators, who historically have worked independently, have become aware that they can learn much from interacting with their peers.

According to Vygotsky (1978), learning is a social process, so classrooms must be social places. Vygotsky says that what we know and are able to do independently can be increased significantly through peer interaction and strong teacher modeling and support. Students need to discuss what they are learning with others. The best classroom environment for struggling readers is one where they can think and talk aloud with their classmates and the teacher about their ideas and questions. The focus of the classroom should not be on the reading itself, but rather on the process of making meaning and creating understandings about content.

If we are to pique the interest of our students, textbooks cannot be their main sources of information—especially for struggling readers. As Moore, Moore, Cunningham, and Cunningham (2003) tell us:

> "Traditional content area textbooks are like freeways. They move you through a lot of territory, but they do it so quickly that you are unable to obtain close, personal insights into the area. In order to genuinely know where you are and have been, you need to exit the freeway and travel the connecting roads. The connecting roads of subject matter are materials such as library books, magazines, newspapers, the Internet, and computer software. These materials provide multiple avenues to thinking and learning." (p. 64)

Let's examine how this might work in class. Instead of beginning a high school science class with, "Open your books and read page 215, then discuss the questions at the end of the chapter," I might start by reading a chapter or two of Richard Preston's *The Demon in the Freezer* (2002), a book about the eradication of smallpox and the threat of biological weapons that provides students with a great deal of vocabulary and new background knowledge. Following the reading, I might ask the students to choose a virus strain to study in teams and then report to the class. Specific instructions on the format, content, and presentation of the reports will guide the teams' work for the rest of the period. In addition to their textbooks, students will use the Internet, scientific articles, magazines, and books on viruses that I have collected for them as sources of information. During the course of the unit, students will also research and conduct a debate on whether the use of biological weapons is ever justified, and write persuasive letters to their representatives in Congress on whether scientists should be allowed to keep active viruses in storage. Because the information is more relevant to current issues and the task gives students a choice in their work, learning will be in-depth, long-term, and meaningful.

We must help students see that reading is the bridge to the ideas in the text. As teachers, we must also understand that textbooks are resources to be read selectively, not cover to cover. If we want students to care about the knowledge we offer, we must show our students how it connects to their world. The sooner we use the textbook as one of many sources, rather than as a sole source, the sooner our students will learn the content we want them to learn.

Student Choice

Allowing students to choose at least some of what they read in class can improve their motivation. Interest inventories can help teachers learn about what interests their students and recommend books accordingly. Remember that success breeds success: Be sure to find a book that the reader can read with at least 95 percent accuracy. (A simple rule of thumb is that if there are more than 7 unknown words among the first 100, the book will probably be too difficult.)

For readers who are several years below grade level, there are many "high interest, low vocabulary" books, and even books on tape for students, available from educational publishers. Many publishers bundle high-interest sets of books together on topics that appeal to both male and female students (e.g. motorcycles, romance). Magazines, the Internet, and picture books can also be great resources for struggling readers. Text that is short and relevant to teens' lives is captivating. The more students simply read, the better readers they will become.

There are many online lists of outstanding books for pre-teens and teens on every topic imaginable, along with reviews and information on authors who are popular with students. The following sources are particularly helpful:

- Carol Hurst Children's Literature Site (http://www.carolhurst.com)

- The Children's Literature Web Guide (http://www.ucalgary.ca/~dkbrown/index.html)

- The BookSpot.com "Teen Reading Lists" Directory (http://www.bookspot.com/features/teenreadinglists.htm)

- The TeenReads.com Web Site (http://www.teenreads.com)

- The Young Adult Library Services Association's "Quick Picks for Reluctant Young Adult Readers" Web Site (www.ala.org/yalsa/booklists/quickpicks)

- The Books for Reluctant Readers Web Site (http://the2rs.com/books_for_reluctant_readers)

All of these Web sites have contributions written for and by kids that can be especially helpful to teachers working with unmotivated students. Teachers should be sure to read the books themselves before purchasing them for class use, however—times have changed regarding what's considered acceptable in teen material. Some books may be appropriate for teens to read outside of school, but not for in-school study and discussion with a whole class. If teachers choose books with controversial content, they should apprise parents of the content prior to using the books with students.

Reader's Theater Productions

Students love Reader's Theater productions, in which they write and perform scripts based on what they read in class. There are many guides to such productions available; one particularly good one is Chris Gustafson's *Acting Cool: Using Reader's Theater to Teach Language Arts In Your Classroom* (2003). There are also many ways to turn content-area materials into scripts: in science class, for example, students could create a performance in which the planets of the solar system are the main characters. Social studies class is filled with wonderful stories that could easily be turned into scripts (see Appendix A for an example).

Poetry Coffee Shops

Another way to make reading fun is to turn your classroom into a version of the local coffee shop, complete with mood lighting. Invite parents, administrators, and fellow teachers to visit your coffee shop, enjoy a brew (even if it is only cocoa), and hear your students practice poems, Reader's Theater presentations, or readings of their own writing. Students love it and present individually, in pairs, or in small groups. The more unusual the material, the better. Some good poetry books are Paul Fleischman's *Joyful Noise* (1988) and *I Am Phoenix* (1985), and of course all of the Shel Silverstein poetry books. Once students get excited about the coffee shop idea, they will find many more books of inspiring or whimsical poems to perform.

Lucky Listener Comment Form

After students have practiced a particular text, have them take a copy of it home and read it to a friend or relative. When they're done reading, they should ask the listener to comment on the reader's rendition by providing feedback and signing a Lucky Listener Comment Form. Once the students have gathered several reactions, have them turn in the comments for extra-credit points. Each signature might get the students a predetermined number of bonus points toward their quarterly grade.

Choral Reading

Have fun with choral readings of text passages or poems. Invite students to get creative with how they read: for example, a poem can be read by having one person start a line, a second person joining in on the second line, a third on the third line, and so forth until the entire class is reading together. Alternatively, the class can begin by reading in unison and then slowly decrease by one or two readers until only one lone voice reads the last line.

Experiment by having individuals, small groups, and the whole class read certain lines to help students hear the lilt of voices responding together like an orchestra. Students can also read by rows, by gender, or by any other category that you can think of to create interest and variety; they will continue to amaze you with new and more creative renditions of pieces that they like to read. The poem "The Cremation of Sam McGee," easily found in children's nursery rhyme books, is one example of a text you might experiment with using different voices and contrasting patterns. Other possibilities from content-area curriculum include the Preamble to the Constitution, Martin Luther King's "I Have a Dream" speech, and the Pledge of Allegiance.

Organizing the Classroom to Meet the Needs of All Readers

Learning is a social process, and adolescents are social creatures who like to talk and interact with their peers. Students learn most from actually "doing" their reading, rather than from drills and worksheets; for this reason, continue reading aloud to your struggling readers whenever possible, even if it is only for five or ten minutes per day. Rasinski (2003) reports that when adults are asked about their most memorable moments in learning to read, "Without question, the number one answer that comes from students is being read to—by a parent, a grandparent, a primary-grade teacher, or other adult. Sometimes students report memories of being read to by a middle- or high-school teacher. These instances might be rare, but they are also among the most memorable and most enriching reading experiences" of older students (p. 19). Hearing adults model fluent reading helps struggling readers and English-language learners to develop an ear for the sounds and flow of the language.

Modeling good oral reading helps students see that the meaning is conveyed not only through the words, but also through the way those words are expressed, grouped, and emphasized. Poor readers often describe "good reading" as reading every word in the sentence without any mistakes. These students are sometimes so concerned with reading each word accurately that they read in a flat, expressionless voice. It is no wonder that when they finish, they have little comprehension of what they've read. Without good phrasing, expression, and pacing, written words bear little resemblance to the spoken ones that students hear in their world.

In addition to poor fluency skills, struggling readers have trouble visualizing what they read. Good readers often visualize such things as the setting, characters, and action described in the text. (This is why we are disappointed with movie versions of novels when the director's interpretation of a scene does not match our own.) Teachers can help struggling students develop visualization skills by asking them to stop and picture what they're reading. Ask them to describe their view of the setting or characters, or to draw a picture of a particularly meaningful scene.

A 1995 study of 4th grade readers sponsored by the U.S. Department of Education (Pinnell et al., 1995) found that students with the best oral reading ability also demonstrated the highest skills in reading comprehension—and that students who struggled with one skill struggled with both. When students must divide their attention between decoding and comprehension, the latter skill is not fully developed—and when they are able to read fluently, their comprehension automatically increases (Rasinski, 2003). Chapter 3 provides you with many ideas to strengthen your students' fluency skills; the rubric in Appendix B can help you measure their progress.

Good modeling, reading material at an appropriate level of difficulty, and choice in the selection of reading material can all improve reading achievement among students. In a study of 2,000 middle school students, Ivey and Broaddus (2001) found that the students' favorite in-class activity was free reading time, during which students were allowed to read material of their own choosing—and their second-favorite activity was read-aloud time. Even older students admitted that being read to made them want to read more on their own. Postlethwaite and Ross (1992) also found a direct correlation between how much teachers encouraged their students to read and student achievement. Krashen (1993) notes that the amount of reading that students do both in school and at home correlates strongly with high classroom achievement.

Book Clubs

Adolescents like to be part of the "in" group and are constantly looking for peer acceptance. A "book club" discussion format can help struggling readers to practice their reading skills while at the same time capitalizing on what they do best—socialize! Knowing that they will be talking about the book with peers, and not wanting to look dumb in front of them, motivates students to complete their reading in time for discussion.

Book clubs take time to develop, however. A teacher cannot simply announce that students will be meeting and discussing books. Teaching students to properly interact in a book club format takes time and proper modeling. Begin by reading to your students and modeling how to ask meaningful questions about the text. Ask open-ended questions about characters, actions, and events that happen in the story: "What do you think of the character of Marney? Is she a nice person?" Other open-ended questions that you might use include: "What strikes you as you read this? What scene did you particularly enjoy reading in this section?" Model your own thoughts and ideas, and get the students to open up about their own impressions. Get students in the habit of referencing page and paragraph for any opinions or comments they make. Ask, "Why do you think this, and what evidence do you have to support your thoughts? Show me something in the book that makes you say this." Opinions should not count unless they can be backed up with evidence from the text.

Asking open-ended questions will help students focus more on the content and meaning of the text and less on the more literal, "What color was the wagon?"–type questions that students have come to expect. Have students respond under your guidance until they master how to answer appropriately. The idea is to help students understand how to discuss a book rather than be the subjects of an inquisition. Once students have a good understanding of how to discuss books in teacher-directed groups, they are ready to move to more student-centered groups under their own leadership.

When moving to student-led discussion groups, begin by selecting several interesting books at different reading levels that focus on a particular concept aligned with your curriculum (e.g., "growing up" or "man against nature"). You can also select books of various reading levels but of the same genre, such as potboilers, biographies, or fantasy. You will need approximately four to six books at various levels of difficulty to accommodate an average-sized class. The Web sites mentioned earlier in this chapter offer some excellent sources for books that older children and teens will likely enjoy.

Introduce each book to the class on the first day of the unit by reciting a short summary that makes the book sound appealing. Place the books on display in the classroom for the remainder of the week so that students can thumb through and look at them. Remind students about the "readability rule": if students encounter 7 unknown words among the first 100 that they read, then the book is probably too difficult for them. At the end of the week, when students have had time to look the books over, ask them each to rank them according to interest. Explain that you will consider many factors in forming the groups, such as who works well together, how the books were ranked, the number of copies of each book available, and so on. Try to place students in a group devoted to one of their top-three book choices whenever possible. Though you should try not to assign students books that you know are way too challenging for them, do not restrict them from reading texts that are only a bit beyond their current reading level if these books are among the students' top choices. Choice and motivation are powerful factors in getting students to read books that are somewhat difficult for them—especially when they will be receiving comprehension help from their peers. By the same token, do not allow advanced readers to regularly select books that are far below their current reading level. After the groups are assigned, ask students to convene and briefly examine their book. Appoint a discussion moderator and a facilitator for each group. The discussion moderator's job is to ask open-ended questions when necessary to stimulate discussion, reminding group members to support their answers with citations from the text. The facilitator's role is to ensure that everyone in the group is participating and no one is dominating the discussion. For the first couple of book club sessions, you might want to choose the moderator and facilitator for each group, although with time the groups should be able to rotate the roles themselves in a sensitive and skillful manner.

Some teachers feel that reading groups work better when each group member is given a role. If you feel this way, consider adding some of the following roles so that each person has a job:

- *Luminary:* Finds interesting, puzzling, or important sections in the text to read aloud to the group.
- *Connector:* Discusses connections between the novel and events in other stories or her own life.
- *Captain:* Organizes the group, ensuring that all members participate and recording important questions that he thinks the group would like to discuss.
- *Character Builder:* Keeps track of observations made about the main characters, listing personality traits and adjectives that describe them, along with supporting page and paragraph citations.
- *Artist:* Responsible for illustrating meaningful elements of the story, such as characters, problems, exciting scenes, predictions, or anything else of interest.
- *Vocabulary Collector:* Searches the text for interesting words, suggesting probable definitions based on the context. Words chosen should be important, unfamiliar, funny, used in an unusual way, or otherwise of note; the student should provide page and paragraph citations for each.

After the ground rules and roles have been set, ask each group to meet briefly to look over its book and set a goal for how much reading it wants to have accomplished before the first discussion. Some teachers have discussion groups once a week, others only every other week. Either way, allow time during the week for students to read their books in class so that they are ready for the discussion. If multiple roles are used, remind students that they will need to gather the information prior to discussion day. If the group chooses a large chunk of reading, it is appropriate for members to read outside of class as well. Tell students upfront exactly how much class time they can expect you to allocate so that they can choose a goal that makes sense for the text length.

As students read the material in preparation for the discussion, ask them to use sticky notes or colorful flags to mark interesting things they find in the text—things that surprised or bothered them or did not seem realistic. They can also mark places where they liked the way something was said, did not understand a word, or did not completely understand what was happening. These notes will help shape the group's discussion. The moderator can follow what you modeled during whole-class discussion by asking students to share any interesting parts they marked. If more specific roles are used, students will be searching for the things you have assigned them to highlight.

Establish early on that students must come to class on discussion day having read the agreed-upon number of pages. There is nothing more frustrating for those who have read their material than to have to endure others trying to wing it during discussion. Tell students that they owe it to their fellow group members to complete their reading goals, and that if for some reason they don't they are to politely excuse themselves from the group to go complete the reading in another part of the room. I guarantee that no student will make that mistake more than once or twice.

Some teachers like to offer their students refreshments, such as popcorn or chips and soda, to make the book discussions more fun and social. Each group gets a small bowl of munchies, finds a place to congregate, and appoints the group's leaders. A list of all leader and participant expectations should be posted on the classroom wall.

Your role is to visit each group and listen in on the discussion and help direct any flailing groups. The livelier the discussion, the more students will like it, and the likelier it is that you'll be asked to clarify a point from the text or add your own opinion. As you circulate, be sure that students are discussing their thinking with their peers and not just offering opinions without evidence from the text. Remind all groups as needed to use examples from the text, citing the specific page and paragraph. One way to keep track of the discussions in each group is to collect the sticky notes that the students used to mark pages and transfer them to each student's reader log or file.

At the end of every discussion, ask each student to rank how well she performed in her role, and ask the group as a whole if it agrees with each self-assessment. Reader support and insight will go a long way toward motivating and helping your most reluctant readers view reading as an enjoyable and socially acceptable activity.

High-Stakes Testing and the Struggling Reader

Learning is a fleeting skill: If we do not use it, we lose it. Like many young, inexperienced teachers, I used to think that my students had never been taught certain skills—in fact, I was convinced that their previous teachers had never even pulled out the district scope-and-sequence for certain subjects. What were they doing all day in those lower grades? When I would begin to introduce, for instance, the concept of multiplying fractions, a glazed look would come over my students' faces; it was as though they had never heard of the idea in their lives. As I was supposed to be teaching the concept at the mastery rather than introductory level, I was amazed that I would have to stop and take time to go over what I thought they should already know.

Wow, was I naïve! In my seventh year of teaching, I had the privilege of moving up a year, or "looping," with my students. When it was time to take the fractions concept I'd taught in the first year a step further in the second year, lo and behold—that same glazed look appeared on their faces! How could this be? I *knew* who their previous teacher had been, and that she'd taught them appropriately.

So much for criticizing *my* lower-level peers ever again. Our brains are just not designed to allow complex concepts to stick; without constant review, students forget what they have been taught. As teachers, we need to connect what we are teaching to prior concepts so that the ideas *do* stick. We also need to help students tie what they learn to something that they can remember: the more senses we involve in learning the ideas, the more likely the brain will be to make connections to the relevant stored data.

According to Vygotsky (1978), we must teach students at a level "just beyond" the one at which they currently function—this is called the "zone of proximal development." If we are teaching at this level, and if we scaffold our instruction so that students can reach the goals we set for them, our students will perform at a higher level than expected on state-mandated tests. If our students have to stretch to reach the expectations set by exams, they will always have trouble passing them.

Over the years, I have seen many teachers dumb down their curriculum and lower their expectations for students. This does no one any favors; research has proven over and over again that students will meet the expectations you set for them. Know the standards and targeted skills that your students are expected to meet, and study sample assessment materials. It is only when you have a good match between curriculum, student, and assessment expectations that successful performance results.

Another pitfall for teachers is thinking that students cannot go on to more interesting projects and higher-level activities because they still have not mastered all of the basics. A good example of this mind-set is the middle school math teacher who keeps her students performing rote basic drills instead of exposing them to the more challenging curriculum of pre-algebra skills specified in their curriculum. The brain operates more efficiently on complexity, so find ways to "fill the holes" with strategic mini-lessons on key skills for struggling students while still exposing them to the curriculum appropriate for their grade level. When students are asked to apply their skills in a meaningful way, their interest and motivation skyrocket. Higher-order thinking skills are perfect for helping students master more basic skills.

Enhancing Reading Comprehension Skills

The Question-Answer Relationship Technique

Struggling readers often do not know how to find answers to questions about the material they read. Even those who can read the assigned text often do not know how to process the material. Raphael's (1984) Question-Answer Relationship technique (QAR) can help teach readers how to locate answers in the text.

The technique categorizes questions as either "in the book" or "in my head" questions. Answers to "in the book" (text-explicit) questions are further separated into "right there" answers, which are explicitly stated in the book, and "think and search" (text-implicit) answers, which require the student to connect two or more pieces of data from the text. Answers in the "in my head" category require students to use their background knowledge in addition to text-based information—to make "on my own" answers to develop a response.

You can best teach students about the three types of questions by modeling an introspective process aloud. Ask the students to do the same—to speak their thoughts as they develop responses to questions—so that you can support them as needed.

Pair Rehearsals

Another good way for students to practice reading is to do so in pairs. Begin by choosing a rehearsal text of an appropriate length and difficulty. To introduce the text to each pair of students, read it to them in a fluent and expressive voice. As you read, clarify anything the students might find confusing, and encourage them to make predictions about what's to come.

When you're done reading, ask the students to reread the text to each other, alternating pages or sections of text as they go, and assisting and coaching each other as necessary. Once the students feel comfortable reading the text as expressively as you did, allow them to present their material to you for feedback. Be sure to provide them with support and encouragement so that they know both what they did well and what they need to work on during the next rehearsal session.

If you have only a few students in the class who need this level of support, tape record a passage of interest and allow the students to practice independently with a headset until they are ready to present the material to you. (You will find more information on tape-recorded practice in Chapters 2 and 4.)

Comprehension is a process, and not an end product. The focus of your instruction with struggling readers should be to help make what is invisible to them visible.

The Highly Disabled Middle or High School Reader

According to Shaywitz (2003), a student who has not received the necessary reading assistance before 3rd grade may need 150 to 300 hours of intensive instruction over a one- to three-year period to close the gap between himself and his peers. This is not a job for peers, classroom instructional aides, volunteers, or teachers who do not possess highly specialized training in reading. High school readers who function at an early elementary reading level require the assistance of highly trained reading specialists; they must have intense, individualized training if they are to bridge the gap and learn effective reading techniques.

Older readers who still have not learned solid decoding skills should not start with phonics instruction, but by learning phonemes, word families, prefixes, and suffixes (Cunningham, 2000). There are 37 phoneme groups that form the basis of nearly 500 words in the English language (Wylie & Durrell, 1970). The "must learn" rimes include the following:

> ack, ain, ake, ale, all, ame, an, ank, ap, ash, at, ate, aw, ay, eat, ell, est, ice, ick, ide, ight, ill, in, ine, ing, ink, ip, ir, ock, oke, op, or, ore, uck, ug, ump, unk

Some other rimes that can also be taught are ab, ace, ade, ail, eam, ent, ew, it, ob, oc, old, ot, and ub. Together, these 50 make up the most common patterns in the English language. When introducing each rime, ask students to make a list of all of the words they can think of that contain the rime in question. List the words provided under the relevant rime on the classroom's Word Wall, so that students can easily see them. Add new words that fit the pattern as they are identified. The more words students look at that contain the rime, the more they will be able to visualize the word formation and the letter patterns. As students learn each rime, hold them accountable for all words that contain this letter sequence in their writing.

Once students understand how to use the concepts of onset and rime to unlock the pronunciation of a word, they can then be taught to use context clues and to remove prefixes and suffixes to decipher words that are new to them. Some helpful strategies to teach patterning and decoding to older readers are provided in the next section. These activities can be used either by reading specialists or by regular Language Arts teachers who have a high number of struggling readers.

Mapping Patterns

Introduce one of the word patterns to the students—the "ain" rime, for instance. Place the rime in the center of a graphic organizer map. Ask students to brainstorm words that can be made from the rime and add them to the organizer map (examples: *train, pain, drain, brain*). As they do this, have them discuss the meaning of the words, and draw a small sketch in each bubble illustrating the meaning. After students have finished their pattern maps, have them create a wall map version with all of the words for continuous display in the classroom. When they're finished, have the students add their individual maps to their vocabulary notebooks.

Fill In the Blanks

Provide students with a list of sentences missing a word, and a list of "demon" words that students often confuse (e.g., *access* and *excess*, *conscience* and *conscious*, *fare* and *fair*). Have the students choose the correct word to fill in each blank. Students should work in pairs or groups of three, so that they can interact and discuss the process. The demon words should also be part of the classroom Word Wall, so that students can see them on a frequent basis.

DISSECT

DISSECT is a word identification strategy by Lenz and Hughes (1990) that helps students decode unknown words. Each letter stands for a different step:

- **D**iscover the context (examine both syntactic and semantic cues)
- **I**solate the prefix (remove it from the root word)
- **S**eparate the suffix (remove it from the root word)
- **S**ay the stem (read the remainder of the word)
- **E**xamine the stem (divide the letters into groups—look for rime patterns or phoneme groups)
- **C**heck with someone for help
- **T**ry the dictionary for assistance

Hidden Rimes

Older successful readers look for rime patterns when reading. Examining the small common rimes in words can help struggling readers become more aware of how rimes fit into longer words. Have students find words that have a particular rime embedded within them—for instance, if the rime is "ight," students might choose words such as *delight, flight,* or *lighthouse.* This activity can also serve to expand student vocabulary.

Timed Rime

Give students a rime pattern that appears in a lot of words, such as "ent." Place the students in teams of three or four and give each group an overhead transparency. Within a given timeframe, ask students to brainstorm all the words they can think of that share the rime—no dictionary or word sources allowed, except for a Word Wall if one is present. Ask them to write the words on the transparency. When you call time, have students read their lists to the class from the overhead projector. Ask another student to record the words, either on the blackboard or on chart paper, as they are listed.

Student teams will receive 1 point for each real word that contains the target rime. No nonsense or foreign words are allowed, and the teacher with a dictionary is the final authority in case of a dispute.

Another way to find rime patterns is to have students look through the newspaper or some other text. See which group can locate the most words with the target rime. Once students have located the words, ask them to create a collage by gluing the words to a piece of paperboard. The collage makes for both a good room decoration and a reminder of the rime pattern being studied.

Word Anagrams

In this exercise, students are asked to create smaller words from the letters in one long word. For example, if the long word is *inventions,* students might come up with words such as *note, sent,* or *invite.*

Getting from Here to There

Get small, blank wall tiles from a tile or hardware store—approximately 100 per student. Using a permanent marker, make three to four copies of consonants and five to six copies of vowels on the tiles by writing one letter per tile. Put the tiles in a large plastic bag for each student, for fast and easy distribution. Ask students to change one word into another word by laying out the starting word with their tiles and then manipulating them according to your step-by-step directions. Example: Start with the word *mat.* Change the *m* to *b.* What word does it make? Change the *a* to *i.* What word does it make? Change only one letter per step to form a new word based on the original word. After students understand the concept, challenge them to "grow" a word by adding one additional letter to the beginning or the end of the word. Example: Start with the word *in.* Add *f* to the word to make *fin;* on the next move, add an *e* to make *fine,* and so on. Challenge groups of students to see who can make the longest chain.

Tell Me a Story

Have pairs of students write a funny paragraph using words that contain a given rime pattern. Example: when learning the "ail" rime, students might write, "Gail took a pail to gather a snail. It started to hail and she stepped on a nail." For a higher level of thinking, students could be given two similar patterns (e.g., "ail" and "ale") and asked to use both correctly in a paragraph. Have students read their stories to the class, and remind them that the more humorous the story, the better.

Sight Words for Older Readers

Although we often teach primary children sight words, learning words in isolation is not particularly helpful, and may even reinforce the idea of word-by-word reading for some students. Reading experts suggest that the phrase is the best unit of study for struggling readers (Schreiber, 1980, 1991; Rasinski, 1990;

Rasinski, Padak, Linek, & Sturtevant, 1994). A good idea is to take some words from a high-frequency word list, such as Fry's "new instant word list" (1980), and organize them into meaningful phrases. Struggling readers should practice these phrases until they can read them smoothly and with good expression.

Because oral reading has been shown to be one of the best indicators of general reading competence (Fuchs, Fuchs, Hosp, & Jenkins, 2001), helping students learn good verbal expression is essential. You can do this by modeling good expression and then coaching students as they read aloud. Struggling readers gain substantially from repeated readings of the same passage with direct feedback and coaching. Some good books for this purpose include Avi's *Something Upstairs* (1990), *Bearstone* by Wil Hobbs (1997), and Mildred Taylor's *The Road to Memphis* (1999). The reading specialist might also ask teachers for words that the students will be expected to recognize in the content areas; by practicing these words as well, students will be better able to keep up with their classroom assignments.

Mystery Word Slates

Tell students that you are thinking of a word from one of their sight word lists, the Word Wall, or a word collection bulletin board. Provide hints such as "My word has five letters" or "My word starts with a consonant." After each hint, ask students to write their guesses on a slate and hold them up for you to see. If the word is guessed after the first clue, the student gets five points; after the second clue, four points; after the third clue, three points; and so on. After the fifth clue, reveal the word and move on to the next one.

Flip Around

Put sight words or phrases up on an overhead transparency, the blackboard, or large sentence strips. Using a pointer, direct students to read each word or phrase chorally in a fast-paced manner. As the class reads together, more skilled students will lead the way as struggling students receive immediate feedback without being put on the spot or embarrassed.

Taking Apart the Word

Write several words on an overhead transparency or on the blackboard. Have students analyze the words and decide as a group how to dissect them into prefixes, suffixes, root words, and rime patterns. Students can use colored markers to indicate the different word parts.

Sight Word Bingo

Make regular 5" x 5" Bingo cards for students. Laminate the cards if possible so that they can be used over and over again with water-soluble markers. Write 24 sight words on the black-board and ask students to write one of the words in each space on their card, leaving the center space empty. Next read each word, asking students to place a bean or plastic marker on the words as they are called. The first person with all the spaces covered in a vertical, horizontal, or diagonal row wins the round. Play can continue till the whole card is covered if desired if more words than spaces are provided.

Sorting Attributes

This is a good activity for English-language learners as well as for struggling readers. On index cards, write various words that you want students to study. Have students work with partners to sort the cards into their own categories (examples: words that have a hard G or C sound, begin with a certain prefix, or contain a particular rime). When students have sorted the cards into the various categories, ask them to explain how the words belong together.

The more students talk through their thinking, the more you can address any misconceptions they may have. You can also use the Sorting Attributes exercise to have students learn various phonic rules, such as the "r-controlled" vowel rule, by identifying instances of the rule when the words are sorted.

It is essential that struggling readers read and talk through the content of assignments with others. This helps them to process and reflect in a productive way on what they know and do not know about the content. Rote learning alone does not work well, so make sure that the students understand the text. It is also very important to help students see that they are making progress: graph fluency rates or comprehension scores so that the students can see that their efforts are paying off in solid increases. Creating benchmarks and celebrating progress will help low-performing readers keep striving to improve their reading skills. Students are much more willing to keep trying when they feel successful and see that they are making progress.

Working with English-Language Learners

Children who speak nonstandard English or who have limited English proficiency when they begin school are also at risk for reading problems. The causes of limited proficiency are many, and intervention at the earliest possible opportunity is the key to preventing reading difficulties that last a lifetime.

State and national accountability standards now hold schools equally accountable for the growth and reading performance of these students despite the language barrier. When students arrive in a country where a different language is spoken, they go through a "silent" period during which they take in the sounds of the language around them (Hakuta & Snow, 1986). This is natural; students need time to absorb the "lilt" of the language. As the need to communicate grows, English-language learners will learn to communicate in a few words and phrases. They may learn words such as *water* or *bathroom* first, as these words are important to survival. In time, their ability to communicate in longer, more complete phrases will develop. Try to de-emphasize oral reading with English-language learners, as it focuses too much on decoding. Work instead on helping them build their vocabulary and comprehension skills. As students' language skills develop, you can then start working on fluency and word pronunciation as needed.

There is a big disparity between the academic performance of English-language learners who are fluent readers in their native language and those who are not (August & Hakuta, 1997). The former usually have had extensive schooling in their home countries, and thus bring a storehouse of solid background knowledge to the classroom. Students from areas with a high emphasis on literacy, such as Europe or Japan, will be likelier to have strong family support for knowledge and learning.

When students come from a literate background, we can quickly present oral language and cognates to which they can relate, since they already have some insight into the purpose and workings of language and reading. When students can read and process at high levels in their own language, they can transfer many of the skills they have already learned to learning a new language; despite different native customs and norms, English-language learners who are already literate can quickly assimilate the norms and practices of their new homeland.

Students who have *not* developed literacy skills in their home countries must gain not just oral language and reading skills, but also extensive background knowledge in content curriculum that other students learned long ago in lower grades.

Because oral language develops before other forms of language, teachers should provide English-language learners with opportunities for a lot of oral interaction, such as through discussions and by participating in small-group work. Talking to other students is motivating, and can encourage students to try harder at communicating with peers.

The English language is filled with slang, idioms, and figurative language. We must help English-language learners to understand vocabulary, word usage, customs, cultural values, and norms. You should discuss and model new information frequently to help these learners develop an ear for the language. Some good books to help students learn about idioms and figurative language are *In a Pickle and Other Funny Idioms* by Marvin Terban (1983) and Fred Gwynne's *Chocolate Moose for Dinner* (1976) and *The King Who Rained* (1970). Students can think about and make their own visual representations of interesting idioms and examples of figurative language based on the ideas in these books.

For beginning speakers, pictures and easy, predictable books can help introduce the sounds and patterns of the English language. Vocabulary cards with pictures on them can also help students expand their vocabulary base. Some older students who are not literate in their own language may not even know how to handle a book. A large amount of oral reading and modeling exactly how to approach a book will help students develop the skills they need. Read predictable books, such as *The Doorbell Rang* (1986) by Pat Hutchins or *The Important Book* (1990) by Margaret Wise Brown, to help English-language learners develop their skills.

Learning about our alphabet is also important, especially when the student's native language uses a different alphabet than we do. Introduce letters to them and have them locate the letters in environmental print in the classroom. Have them match words to pictures, or create "personal dictionaries" in which to write words they want to remember, together with their own definitions of the words. Activities such as echo reading and choral reading of poems, songs, and predictable text will also help English-language learners who are not literate in their first language to better learn English. Writing must be seen as a means of expression and idea generation, with mechanics emphasized only after students have learned the basics of getting their ideas down on paper. Graphic organizers are very helpful to English-language learners, as the visual representation helps them see relationships and identify key concepts and connections.

Online Resources

A good Web site for information about working with English-language learners is http://www.eslkidstuff.com. Another site, http://www.escort.org, run by the State University of New York at Oneonta, offers a free, downloadable guide called *Help! They Don't Speak English Starter Kit* in its "Products" section. (The guide is large, so either download with a high-speed connection or expect to wait a long while.) The Internet is also an excellent resource for free pictures to use in building vocabulary. Parent volunteers or even students themselves can cut out the pictures and mount them on index cards for easy and repeated use.

To get small paragraphs translated either from English or into English for some of the more common languages, try http://www.freetranslation.com. This site supports translation software for Spanish, French, German, Italian, Dutch, Portuguese, Norwegian, simplified Chinese, and traditional Chinese.

Many foreign students are shy about speaking and worried about making mistakes in their use of language, so respect their need for time and processing of English words and phrases. The classroom environment must be supportive, fun, and encouraging. Students must feel that it is acceptable to make a mistake and take risks without being laughed at or ridiculed. When they feel supported, they will take greater risks to expand their learning.

Many teachers confuse social language proficiency with academic proficiency. I have often heard teachers say things such as, "He talks to other students just fine, but he has trouble with academics." Just because students can communicate at a conversational level does not mean that they can understand the language used for content-area teaching and sophisticated sentence construction. There is a three- to five-year lag between the time it takes students to easily communicate at a social level versus at an academic level (Cummins, 1994).

When students arrive from another country, their focus has to change from learning content to communicating in a new language. Cummins reminds us that while English-language learners are acquiring language skills, their native-speaker peers are progressing in their knowledge of the content areas. Thus English-language learners must "catch up with a moving target" if they are to match the proficiency levels of native speakers. This is difficult for even the brightest of students, so we must be patient and supportive of their learning.

Be sure to encourage classmates to be supportive of one another and to provide many opportunities for English-language learners to practice their new skills without being the center of attention. Maintain a positive, supportive classroom climate in which all students feel included. Little by little, the English-language learners' skills and self-confidence will grow, and you will find them taking more and more risks in their speaking. Allow them the freedom to listen, think, process, and respond when they can, and they will grow much faster.

Struggling Readers Can Succeed

Supportive classrooms where students can experience success with teachers skilled in teaching reading are key to helping all students prepare for the literacy demands they will face in society. To prevent reading difficulties, teachers must monitor students regularly and give them targeted support as soon as they begin to fall behind their age-level benchmarks. Once students fall behind, intensive and directed support will be necessary to help them close the gap. Content-area teachers must examine how they make meaningful connections for their students. When all teachers take responsibility for developing good reading skills in all students, student success rates will soar.

2 | Fluency

Fluency is the ability to read a text accurately, smoothly, and quickly, with expression, proper phrasing, and good comprehension. Students who read a particular text fluently have developed what is known as "automaticity" (Samuels, 1994) with the material they are reading. They also have good vocabularies and word identification skills, and can draw connections between the text and their own background knowledge (Armbruster, Lehr, & Osborn, 2001). As Hirsch (2003) states, "Prior knowledge about the topic speeds up basic comprehension and leaves working memory free to make connections between the new material and previously learned information, to draw inferences, and to ponder implications. A big difference between an expert and a novice reader—indeed between an expert and a novice in any field—is the ability to take in basic features very fast, thereby leaving the mind free to concentrate on important features" (p. 13).

Fluency develops over time and varies according to the material being read. It is not a "stage" of development; rather, it varies with the difficulty of the text, as well as the reader's familiarity with the text and background knowledge of its content. There is a strong correlation between how fast you can read a text and how well you can understand it. Those who can process text at a level of automaticity can direct more conscious attention to the text's meaning than to decoding the words. When text processing is quick and easy, the working memory is free to think about what the text actually means and to process it at deeper levels of understanding. The more the brain can concentrate on making meaning, the more the reader will comprehend the content.

There are two types of fluency: oral fluency and silent reading fluency. *Oral fluency* deals with prosodic features such as stress, pitch, expression, intonation, and text phrasing. Being able to demonstrate oral fluency does not necessarily mean that one is a fluent reader—we have all seen students who can read out loud with speed, expression, and smooth decoding but can't comprehend the material. *Silent reading fluency* is achieved when we have enough automaticity with the decoding process to be able to focus on comprehending the text while reading silently and independently. Both sets of skills are necessary but are not developed in the same ways. Rasinski (2003) suggests that "silent reading should take on a more prominent role as students move up the grades," but that "oral reading should continue to play a prominent role as well, because it leads to better silent reading" (p. 8).

As adults, we have all had the pleasure of struggling through a text that makes no sense to us—a contract, for instance, or a mandatory textbook in a challenging subject. Such difficulty is due to the text being beyond our level of fluency. Perhaps the vocabulary is unfamiliar to us, or the writing is convoluted, or we're not interested or knowledgeable enough in the subject. These problems force us to slow our reading pace and struggle with comprehension.

As capable readers, we have learned many strategies to increase comprehension, such as slowing down our reading pace, rereading the text, or reading material aloud. We may ask questions about the material, or ask more expert readers whether we have properly understood the text. Clarification helps us understand and extract the meaning we need.

Struggling readers sometimes assume that they should approach all text in the same manner, whether it is a comic book or a textbook. This assumption can contribute to a sense of help-lessness—when presented with a reading challenge, many students simply give up altogether. Students need to be taught that good readers approach text in different ways when the going gets tough. By modeling and thinking aloud ourselves, we can help them learn these skills.

Hirsch (2003) tells us that it usually "takes several years of decoding practice before children can process a printed text as rapidly as they can process that same text when listening to it" (p. 12). Fluency marks the transition point between learning to read and being able to understand text. Unfortunately, not all students are reaching this point: The National Center for Educational Statistics (2001) recently reported that 45 percent of all 4th graders tested in the United States are not fluent readers. Without this solid weave in the tapestry of reading, we cannot expect students to develop strong understandings of academic content and expository text.

The Stages of Reading Development

Chall (1996) proposes six stages through which readers pass as they develop into mature, effective readers. The first is the early reading or emergent literacy stage, during which readers develop foundational skills, insights into the reading process, and knowledge about print and book-handling concepts. They also learn about the connections between sounds and language and develop a sense of phonemic awareness. At this stage, readers learn that print represents language and that it carries the message of the story.

At stage 2, formal reading instruction begins, with an emphasis on sound-symbol correspondences and establishing basic decoding skills and accuracy. It is at this stage that readers learn to decode print and read text out loud.

In stage 3, readers develop decoding automaticity—what Chall calls "ungluing from print" (1996). At this stage, readers learn to use appropriate text phrasing, pitch, stress, and intonation while reading. Solid fluency begins to emerge at stages 3 and 4, and attention shifts to making meaning from the words rather than just decoding them. All readers should develop fluency, expression, and strong word-recognition skills at this stage before moving on. For most students, stage 3 signals a change from reading narrative text ("learning to read") to processing more informational or expository text ("reading to learn").

In proficient readers, stage 4 is a transitional stage, beginning somewhere around the end of 2nd grade and continuing through the 5th or 6th grade. For struggling readers, it may be even longer. At this level, readers should readily display adequate levels of automaticity, fluency, and comprehension, and are expected to master increasingly complex material while processing much longer textual passages. Readers should be exposed to increasing amounts of content-rich, expository text, such as textbooks. Much of the text is presented from only a single perspective and in an introductory manner. Some students who have been progressing well up to this point will begin to struggle with vocabulary and comprehension skills in stage 4.

Readers in stage 5 begin to draw critical judgments, interpretations, and comparisons with regard to the text—in other words, they become independent thinkers. The sixth and final stage of literacy development is the "multiple viewpoints" stage. At this level, readers can process and analyze text containing multiple viewpoints, express their own opinions about the content and author's viewpoint, critically evaluate the sources cited in the text, and evaluate ideas and viewpoints from the perspective of related texts that they've read.

According to Chall, readers in stage 6 develop "construction and reconstruction" skills. The sixth stage is what the National Assessment of Educational Progress refers to as the advanced level—it's where we ideally want every high school reader to be upon graduating. Stage 6 readers can analyze the author's writing style, the development and organization of the text, and the narrative's main points. This stage forms the foundation for the activities described in the higher-order literacy thread in Figure I.1 of the Introduction. Success at this level is the ultimate goal of our instruction.

How Can We Develop Reading Fluency?

Reading expressively helps to hold our attention. When we read orally, we chunk words into meaningful groups, vary the pitch and the intonation patterns of our voice, place stress on some words but not on others, and punctuate our speech with pauses and rising inflections to indicate thought breaks or questions. Effective oral readers can also transfer these skills to silent reading. This is what makes being curled up in our favorite chair with a good book so much fun: we can "hear" in our minds the comments and discussions that occur between our favorite characters. Similarly, we can chuckle to ourselves at the clever limericks and humorous situations we read because we can hear the "melody" of the language as we read with expression in our "mind's ear."

Unfortunately, classroom teachers sometimes take fluency for granted and neglect to teach the relevant skills directly to their students. As Chall's six stages suggest, refinement of fluency skills is at the center of the transition from basic decoding to critical reading. Without fluency, comprehension is limited. There are four effective ways to develop and strengthen fluency skills in students:

- Modeling and direct feedback,
- Extensive reading practice,
- Repeated readings of a single text, and
- Practice with specific components of fluency such as pace, expression, and chunking.

We will examine each of these methods separately.

Modeling and Direct Feedback

For students to become fluent readers, they must hear good models of what fluent reading sounds like and be able to imitate them. Teachers should model smooth, expressive reading by reading aloud to students daily, even if only for 5 to 10 minutes. Although this practice is common in the lower grades, most upper-grade teachers have not been trained to include daily oral reading into their lesson plans. With burgeoning populations of English-language learners and struggling readers in our classrooms, we can no longer ignore the importance of modeling.

Students, especially those with a limited oral reading background, must understand that reading is just written speech; until they make this realization, they will have trouble making the connection between the conversations they hear every day and the words they read. If students are not fluent readers by the time they reach the beginning of 4th grade, they must begin to practice print as "written talk" so that they can emphasize meaning rather than decoding. It is difficult to monitor meaning and think critically when you are still stumbling over the words in an effort to decode them.

Fluency instruction and oral reading activities are especially helpful for English-language learners. Through oral reading practice, classroom discussions, and frequent reading rehearsal, such students can practice intonation, language rhythm, stress, and pacing. Be sure to show students what fluent and nonfluent reading sounds like, model the difference between smooth and choppy reading, teach the difference between monotonous and expressive reading, and demonstrate how good readers alter the volume, speed, and pitch of their voice to make stories more interesting for listeners.

There are many other ways that teachers can support daily fluency instruction. In Language Arts or Social Studies classrooms, students can practice poems, rehearse plays, or participate in Reader's Theater, to name just a few strategies. These types of performance-based opportunities allow students to work on their expression, delivery, and intonation in a guided yet interesting environment; the process of polishing and delivering the script for an audience becomes the reader's focus. The teacher acts as the "stage director" or "producer," coaching the actors to improve their delivery. Chris Gustafson's *Acting Cool! Using Reader's Theater to Teach Language Arts and Social Studies in Your Classroom, Grades 5–7* (2003) is an especially good source of ideas for short pieces that complement language arts or social studies lessons. The monthly magazine *Plays* also offers a variety of plays that 4th–12th grade students will enjoy rehearsing and performing for their classmates; copies can be obtained at http://www.playsmag.com.

When oral renditions are used in the classroom, provide feedback to students on how they deliver their lines. Ask students to describe the way particular students or groups rendered specific passages, to heighten their awareness of variability in delivery. Keep your comments positive and encouraging so that students will want to participate again and again. Highlight what was done well, and encourage students to identify effective delivery techniques that they can employ in their own performances.

Teachers can also have students interview "experts" in their content area, with one student acting as the interviewer and another as the guest expert. Another option is for students to gather evidence and argue a side of a controversial issue and stage a debate, court hearing, or legislative inquiry.

Here are a few additional exercises to enhance oral performance through modeling and feedback.

Whose Voice?

Put a sentence or two or a paragraph on the overhead projector or blackboard. Ask students to read the text using different perspectives or voices. For example: How would a kindly grandmother read the lines? How about a sumo wrestler or a stern father? Students will enjoy creating these new perspectives. You can extend the idea by helping them dramatize scenes using a specific dialect, or by changing the characters in the story (turning Juliet into a Valley girl, for instance, or Macbeth into a 1930s gangster). This type of practice can help teach the concept of voice.

Focused Practice

Provide students with a general text that can be used for several types of fluency activities. Ask students to read the text a few times, concentrating on a different reading purpose each time. For example, the first reading might focus on good expression, the second on reading punctuation appropriately, the third on phrasing or intonation, or improving silent reading speed. This strategy helps students understand that there are different components to fluency, and repeated readings of a text can improve both comprehension and reading ability.

Fractured Fairy Tales

If you are old enough to remember the "Rocky and Bullwinkle" TV cartoon, you probably remember the "Fractured Fairy Tales" segment. This involved a traditional fairy tale told from a new perspective. Books such as Jon Scieszka's *The True Story of the Three Little Pigs!* (1989) and *The Stinky Cheese Man and Other Fairly Stupid Tales* by Scieszka and Lane Smith (1992) explore the same concept, and can be read to students as models. Once you've presented students with examples, ask them to rewrite their favorite fairy tale or scene from a new perspective. How would the wolf in "Little Red Riding Hood" tell the story? How would Prince Charming narrate "Cinderella"?

Language Ebb and Flow

Have students listen carefully as you read aloud to them. Demonstrate the rise and fall of the sentences by moving your hands up and down with the flow, or by marking them with upward or downward pen strokes on an overhead transparency as you speak. When students have grasped the concept of sentence flow, have them practice reading a passage with a partner, who should indicate how she thinks the flow should be read and signal as much with her hands while the other person reads. This technique is especially helpful for English-language learners who need to become attuned to the lilt of spoken English.

History in the Making

Ask students to create a skit about a historical event from their social studies text. If additional information is needed for the skit, provide reference materials or Internet resources. Students can create a Reader's Theater, a short play, or simply a dialogue between two historical characters. They might also pretend to be reporters on the scene interviewing famous historical figures. The students will enjoy being creative and will learn a lot of content in the process. Once students have practiced their skits well enough, you might even want to consider taking the show on the road to other classrooms.

Old-Time Radio Plays

You can find tapes of old-time radio plays such as "The Shadow" in bookstores or on the Internet. Ask students to listen to one of the tapes and study how the actors use expression, tone, and pauses to make their presentation more interesting to the listener. Have students rehearse and record their own "radio plays" using what they've learned from studying the professional tapes; they might even add music or sound effects to their presentations, which can be offered to other classes for their enjoyment as well.

Choral Control

Reader's Theater pieces or poems with stanzas are great ways for struggling readers to practice reading without embarrassment. Appoint different groups to chorally read a section or stanza from a text while modeling as much expression as possible. Provide feedback to the group each time the piece is read. A good text for this exercise is *Silly Salamanders and Other Slightly Stupid Stuff for Reader's Theater* by Fredericks and Stoner (2000). For older readers, try *Folktales on Stage* (2003) and *Stories on Stage* (1993) by Aaron Shepard, *Take Ten: New 10-Minute Plays* (1997) by Lane and Shengold, or *Thirty Ten-Minute Plays for Two Actors* (2001) by Dixon, Wegener, and Petruska. For kids or teachers who enjoy Shakespeare, try *Welcome to the Globe: The Story of Shakespeare's Theatre* (2000) by Peter Chrisp. Web sites that offer Reader's Theater scripts include http://www.aaronshep.com/rt/, http://www.teachingheart.net/readerstheater.htm, and http://www.eplaybooks.com, a commercial script vendor.

Reading Buddies

Ask struggling readers to serve as reading buddies to younger students. Partner with a primary classroom and assign each student one or two buddies to work with once or twice per week. Help students select appropriate picture books for the young reader's age and sex. Ask students to practice reading the selected book to each other so that they can read it in an entertaining manner to their buddies. During the practice sessions, students give each other suggestions on how they can better deliver the material so as to create interest in their younger listeners.

Shared Performances

When students complete final rehearsals of quality performances, place their scripts in a classroom learning center for others to review. Other students may want to try to interpret the same material differently, or try to improve upon the original performance, as actors do when they remake an old movie.

Taped Feedback

Teachers can use taped passages as a way to evaluate student fluency development. Students can also take turns using a rubric to score one another on their playbacks, with the emphasis on identifying what the fellow student does well rather than on criticism.

What Comes Next?

Good readers anticipate words that come next in a sentence before they actually read them. One good activity for strengthening this skill is to take a passage with fairly predictable content and good context clues and block out certain key words here and there. As students read the text, ask them to anticipate what word the author might have used next. Any word the student suggests, as long as it's grammatically correct and fits structurally into the paragraph, is acceptable. Because the purpose of the activity is to develop sensitivity to context clues, it does not matter whether the word is actually the one the author used; what matters is just that it's appropriate for the context.

Extensive Reading Practice

Researchers have noted that reading practice has a positive effect on fluency (Dowhower, 1987; Samuels, 1979): the more students read, the more fluent they become. According to the National Reading Panel (2000), guided oral reading and repeated reading of the same text was found to be effective across multiple grade levels.

Despite the direct benefits of practice, many adolescent readers actively avoid reading because they find it difficult, slow, and frustrating (Ackerman & Dykman, 1996; Cunningham & Stanovich, 1997). As Louisa Moats (2001) points out:

> Therein lie the most challenging aspects of teaching older students: they cannot read, so they do not like to read; reading is labored and unsatisfying, so they have little reading experience; and because they have not read much, they are not familiar with the vocabulary, sentence structure, text organization, and concepts of academic "book" language. Over time, their comprehension skills decline because they do not read, and they also become poor spellers and poor writers. What usually begins as a core phonological and word recognition deficit, often associated with other language weaknesses, becomes a diffuse, debilitating problem with language—spoken and written. (p. 37)

We must find ways to hook students on reading so that this vicious cycle of reading avoidance can be broken.

Contrary to what many teachers think, the "round-robin" strategy of reading instruction is one of the least effective ways of building students' reading skills. According to Eldredge, Reutzel, and Hollingsworth (1996), round-robin techniques improve neither student fluency skills nor comprehension abilities, because they only require students to read small, specific passages of text. As soon as the teacher moves on to another reader, the reader who just took a turn is no longer accountable and may stop paying attention. As most of us who have been subjected to this type of practice know, many students dread round-robin reading. More effective readers will often "count ahead" to determine which passage they will need to read and silently rehearse it a few times so that they will be prepared when called upon. Most of us probably did this as students ourselves. But when struggling readers provide their renditions in a halting, stumbling way, more advanced readers might find themselves reading rather than listening to the passage in order to understand what was being said—or worse, simply ignoring it. Most teachers keep moving without clarifying much about the text, regardless of student fluency. There are several more effective approaches to classroom content area reading than the round-robin method, so I hope you will consider dropping this ineffective practice for one that provides students with more positive and productive reading support.

One effective strategy is called "Read and Reflect." In this method, the teacher reads a short section of the text aloud for students, stopping after a few paragraphs to lead the class through an in-depth discussion of what's been read. The teacher asks students to summarize and restate key points in their own words: "Who can summarize what we just read about?" Students provide key details and are allowed to ask questions and seek clarification on anything that confuses them. They could also complete graphic organizers or make notes in their content reading logs about what they are learning. The teacher then reads the next section of text, and the process is repeated. This emphasis on understanding the text and summarizing what has been heard helps everyone focus on meaning rather than their own reading performance.

Another approach to more effective processing of content-area text materials is to assign a section of text to a group of three or four students to read and prepare. Have the students read the passage, ask one another clarifying questions, and interpret key information in their own words. Each group then prepares a short class presentation on the material to teach the key points to their peers. Other students can ask for clarification on key points from the "experts" and are responsible for taking accurate notes on the information. This strategy involves students at a concrete level of understanding and provides a focus for learning. Because the students are responsible for both presenting and clarifying the information, understanding of and interest in the subject matter improve. (Additional strategies for effectively involving students in reading activities can be found in Chapter 5.)

As students progress through school, they have less and less time for classroom reading. We must find ways of making time in school for students to read what interests them. One of the biggest problems that teachers have is finding books that interest intermediate and high school students. When they are motivated, students will persist at a task despite minor difficulties. The more students read, the more their reading improves—and the more their reading improves, the more they will be willing to read. When the task becomes easy as well as enjoyable, fluency and reading skills skyrocket and the student is able to progress to Chall's Stage 5 or 6.

When we ask students to read for practice, we should try to ensure that the material is challenging but not too difficult. Allington (2001) recommends that students practice on materials with which they have at least a 95 percent accuracy rate. "High interest, low vocabulary" books are available to ensure that readers have some level of background knowledge and interest in the material, as well as success with its structure and vocabulary. Male and female readers have different tastes in reading material. Eighty percent of the books females buy are fiction, whereas the reverse is true for males (Cunningham, Hall, & Gambrell, 2002).

The Web site of the American Library Association, http://www.ala.org, provides links to lists of books that will interest students of all ages. For the association's annual rankings of the "Best Books for Teens," see http://www.ala.org/yalsa/booklists/bbya; books that will interest more reluctant readers are listed at http://www.ala.org/yalsa/booklists/quickpicks. I've also listed a few good options on the "links" page of my Web site, http://www.threadsofreading.com. Make it a goal to expose students to all kinds of text—from fiction to expository to persuasive to technical. The more students are familiar with all types of text, the better readers they will become.

Repeated Readings of a Single Text

For struggling readers or English-language learners, rehearsal and feedback on the performance of reading passages is essential. Practicing on a single text is an excellent technique to help these students improve their fluency skills (Samuels, 1979). Give struggling readers a text that is slightly above their independent reading level, and match them with helpful partners. Ask one student in each pair to read a portion of the text while the other student listens. When the reader is done reading the portion, the partner offers feedback on what the reader did well. The reader should then continue reading, keeping in mind the positive feedback. After a few passages, the roles should be reversed.

Coaching should always support and encourage a reader, and should never dishearten those who are already struggling. Be sure that all partners understand the ground rules and that you have modeled giving positive and helpful feedback before you allow students to coach one another.

Echo Reading

Another effective strategy that teachers can use with individuals, pairs, or small groups is "echo reading." Choose a fluent reader to read a sentence and model good fluency, then have the other students attempt to read it in exactly the same way. After a couple of times reading the material together, ask each student to read the passage on his or her own. You can use an overhead projector, or put the phrases on cards, and reveal one passage at a time to help students better group into appropriate clusters the words they are reading .

High-Interest Reading

Ask a struggling reader to select a book, short story, or magazine article that interests him. It does not matter if the material is
too difficult as long as it is something the student really wants to
learn to read. Have a fluent adult reader read a 5–10 minute segment of the student's chosen text slowly into a tape recorder
(approximately 75–100 words per minute). The tape should not
have sound effects or music. Then have the student listen to the
material, preferably with a headset, and ask him to follow along
silently with the text as it is being read. After listening to the tape
a few times, the student should read out loud along with the
speaker on the tape. Ask the student to continue practicing the
text with the taped voice until he can fluently read it independently without the tape. When the student feels that he can read
the material well, have him read the material to you or to another
fluent reader, who in turn should provide positive feedback and
coaching as needed.

In a study by Smith and Elley (1997), struggling students who
repeatedly listened to high-interest stories on tape until they could
read them successfully on their own progressed by an average of
2.2 years in only 27 weeks. They even maintained the gains during
the two-month summer break. Similarly, Koskinen and Blum (1999)
reported substantial growth among English-language learners who
read along with high-interest tapes both at school and at home.

A rubric to judge your students' progress on fluency development is provided in Appendix B.

Practicing Specific Skills: Expression, Phrasing, Chunking, and Speed

In addition to modeling and practice, educators need to directly
teach fluency development skills to students. When students are
just beginning to learn to read, their speech is sometimes flat or
monotone: because they are devoting so much energy to

decoding, they have little left to consider how the words might actually be spoken. The less effort is needed for decoding, the sooner students will start reading with expression.

When students are first learning to read sentences, they have little understanding of how to "chunk" the words of the sentence into meaningful groups. Chunking helps students improve comprehension, as they are not trying to process entire sentences at once. Learning how sentences are organized is especially important for English-language learners, who need to develop a feel for their new language. Help them learn to chunk sentences so that they flow smoothly and make sense.

Before reading, good readers consider the type of material being read, its purpose, the degree of understanding needed, and their level of motivation for reading the text. Is the material a comic strip read purely for enjoyment, or is it a scholarly text being read to prepare for a university class test? We must teach students that knowing the purpose and type of a text helps us determine how fast we should read it. Ask students to practice reading at various speeds—from skimming to attentive—so that that they know what each speed entails. The skill of reading at varied speeds must be discussed and directly taught to students. Struggling readers often do not know that good readers vary their reading rate according to the purpose of the text. Because they attack all print in the same halting way, it does not occur to them that this is not how all readers process text. We must help these students understand the intricacies of purpose.

Learning to read faster is a skill that must be practiced to be improved. An average 4th grade student should be able to read around 130–150 words per minute (wpm), an 8th grader around 210–220 wpm, and a high school senior around 260–280 wpm. Charting student reading speeds can help students focus on developing this skill.

To practice fluency speed, students should start by reading fairly easy material as fast as they can while still maintaining the ability to retell what they have read or answer basic comprehension questions about the material. To find a student's reading rate, divide the number of words in the passage by the time needed to read the passage. Periodically working on improving reading speed helps to improve overall reading rates. Have students graph the results on a chart so they can see the improvement themselves. Being able to process text quickly and efficiently motivates students to read by making the task seem doable; no one wants to tackle a monumental task that will take hours and hours of painful struggle. A slow reader who laboriously works to get through each page of a novel will likely not even want to begin the two-inch thick book in front of her. If we are to help our students enjoy reading, students must be successful and reading must be seen as pleasurable.

The following strategies can help students develop good foundational skills for fluency.

Talk, Talk

Find books with extensive passages of dialogue and have students discuss how they think each speaker would have said his or her part. Practice reading the conversations in different ways. How does the meaning or interpretation change? What might the character have been thinking or feeling as the words were said? What clues led you to think this?

Paragraph Perspectives

Show students groups of sentences or paragraphs that can be punctuated in different ways depending on the intended meaning. Example: "Mary Kate, our neighbor, arrived home at two" versus "Mary Kate, our neighbor arrived home at two." Ask students to place slash marks between words that can be grouped together and have them read the sentences with the pauses indicated. Discuss the meaning of the sentence with the pauses in the current positions. Then move the slash marks and discuss how the meaning has changed.

Though difficult, this activity is very helpful for English-language learners and struggling readers. Neither group has developed finely honed sensitivities to punctuation, so be sure to have students work in groups so that more able readers can help them understand subtle differences in meaning. Another version of this activity is to examine how placing the stress on different words changes the meaning of the sentence.

Step It Up

Locate simple passages of one to four paragraphs for students to read at their independent reading level (no more than five to seven errors per 100 words). Encourage students to read the passage as fast as they can while still maintaining comprehension. Have a partner time the student and determine his or her reading rate (number of words divided by reading time). At the end of the reading, the student must be able to list the Five Ws—who, what, where, when, and why—of the passage. If students are able to list the information accurately, they can graph the latest reading rate on their personal rate logs. If they are not able to do so, they must slow down, reread the passage, and try again.

Phrase Markers

Give student pairs paragraphs of dialogue and ask them to consider how the text should best be delivered. Have them mark the text with up and down arrows and pause marks according to how they think it should be read for maximum interest. Have them practice reading the text until they can deliver it smoothly and effectively per their markings. If the markings do not help the delivery, instruct the students to change the text markers. This process will help students think about good expression and the changes that take place in spoken language.

Faster, Faster

In some speed reading programs, students are taught to place a finger down the centerline of a text and "flash" their eyes from left to right at the text on both sides of the finger. The reader then moves the finger down to the next line in a slow but steady manner to keep the reading flow going. This encourages taking in multiple words in groups rather than fixating on each word individually. While this exercise takes some practice, it can substantially increase student reading rates. As with the "Step It Up" technique, the test of this process is whether the reader can relate the Five Ws of the passage; if not, he should move the finger more slowly down the center of the page. Use very easy text for practice to increase reading speed.

Hearing While We Read

When we first learn to read as small children, we often need to do so aloud to maintain comprehension. This is because so much of our brain is simply working on decoding and visual discrimination; we do not have enough processing capacity or skill to maintain comprehension without "hearing ourselves talk" as we read. Many of us, however, have maintained a related habit of "listening to the words" in our heads when we read silently. Though this habit impedes our reading speed by limiting it to the speed at which we "talk" in our heads, it can be helpful when the text is difficult and a high degree of comprehension is required.

To break the habit of constantly "reading in the head," start by placing a card above the text. Bring the card down the page slowly, hiding the line that was just read as the card is lowered. Work on flashing the eyes across the line from left to right while taking in groups of words rather than individual ones before the card covers them. Try to concentrate on getting the gist of the text rather than stopping to understand and process each word. Again, the test of success is whether the reader can determine the Five Ws upon completion of the reading.

If this is too much to learn at once, cut out a window in a card large enough to view two to three words at a time. Slide the card across the line so the reader can see one group of words at a time. Try to take in the whole group as one segment without hearing the words in your head. Try to keep the window moving steadily across the text as quickly as possible while still maintaining comprehension. You will be surprised at how much you will retain of the material at the end of the practice time.

Try to practice this window-card technique when the text is easy and being read for enjoyment. Students will find that the strategy helps them skim content quickly and efficiently when they need to locate specific data. The window-card exercise is especially helpful for dyslexic readers, many of whom have not developed good eye tracking for reading. Don't worry about struggling readers increasing their speed until they have mastered the fluency stage altogether. If placing the card over the text is a problem for students, have them place it below the text and pull the card down as they go. Encourage students not to reread any passages they have already read.

Putting on the Pause

Students need to think about phrasing and grouping words into expressive thoughts as they read. To practice this skill, provide a paragraph with double spaces between each word. Ask students to think about how the paragraph should be read and where the reader should pause while reading. Have them place slash marks wherever they think the reader should pause, and then read their interpretations to partners for feedback. Ask the class to decide where they think the pauses have the greatest effect for the listener.

Fluency: The Bridge to Effective Reading

Good fluency provides a bridge from basic decoding to comprehension. To learn to read fluently and with good expression, students have to hear good models and practice strong fluency skills. These skills are absolutely necessary if our students are to progress to the high levels of critical and creative thinking that they will need for future success.

3 | Vocabulary

Vocabulary consists of the words that we understand and can actively listen to, speak, read, or write. According to Snow and colleagues (1998), we all have four different vocabularies: the listening vocabulary, the speaking vocabulary, the reading vocabulary, and the writing vocabulary. The listening vocabulary develops first, followed by the speaking vocabulary, the reading vocabulary, and the writing vocabulary, in that order. The size of each vocabulary depends on the individual—for instance, people who read extensively may have a particularly large reading vocabulary. Each vocabulary expands throughout an individual's life, with time and consistent use. We will concentrate on the reading and writing vocabularies as they are most often associated with success in school.

Vocabulary is a vital foundational thread in the tapestry of reading; it should be woven into the fabric of everything that is being studied. Most students add approximately 2,000–3,000 words per year to their reading vocabularies, or about 6 to 8 new words per day (Anderson & Nagy, 1992). Reading only 10 minutes per day can result in students learning about 1,000 new words each year (Cunningham & Stanovich, 1998). The larger one's spoken vocabulary, the easier it is to decode words in text.

All upper grade teachers are aware of huge differences in the vocabularies of their students. It is, in fact, one of the big differences between proficient and struggling readers (Baker, Simmons, & Kameenui, 1995). Many struggling readers have moderately large listening vocabularies, because listening is their main way of taking in information, but relatively undeveloped reading and writing vocabularies. For these students, building all four vocabularies from when they first enter school must be a high priority.

A high-performing 1st grade student knows roughly twice as many words as the low-performing 1st grade student, and the gap only increases over the years. By 12th grade, high-performing students know approximately four times as many words as their low-performing peers (Graves, Brunetti, & Slater, 1982).

Gaps in Vocabulary Established Early in Life

The number of words in a vocabulary is directly proportional to the amount of language that a child has been exposed to early in life. A longitudinal study of language development by Hart and Risley (1995, 2003) showed that the amount of language that children are exposed to from birth on is associated with the extent of a child's vocabulary by the age of 3 or 4. The researchers studied parents and children in 42 families from three socioeconomic backgrounds—white-collar, working-class, and low-income—and tracked parent-child verbal interactions in the home from the time the child was 7–9 months old through the early preschool years. According to Hart and Risley, "The data showed that ordinary families differ immensely in the amount of experience with language and interaction they regularly provide their children and that differences in children's experience are strongly linked to children's language accomplishments at age 3" (2003, p. 2). The data clearly showed that by 34–36 months, children's vocabularies correlated with those of their parents. For example, in white-collar families, parents used an average of 487 words per hour and children an average of 310, whereas working-class parents and their children used an average of 301 and 223 words per hour respectively.

Several low-income families also participated in the study. The comparison with white-collar families is startling: In the low-income families, parents used an average of 176 words per hour, and children 168 words per hour. Extrapolated out to the age of 4, this shows that children from white-collar families would be exposed to approximately 45 million words, and children in low-income families to only 13 million words—a vocabulary gap of some 32 million words.

Hart states that when some of these children were retested at ages 9 and 10, the same vocabulary gap was still evident despite the added factor of school attendance. Additional studies (Graves, Brunetti, & Slater, 1982; White, Graves, & Slater, 1990) reinforce the observation that 1st, 2nd, and 3rd grade children from high-income families have 30 to 50 percent larger vocabularies than do lower-income children.

For students who are learning English as a second language, the vocabulary gap is a huge chasm that can prevent effective learning and strong academic performance. Only with an intensive effort to expand vocabulary skills can struggling readers and English-language learners develop in the other threads of reading. It is clear that this effort cannot stop at any point for these children. Without it, they will have difficulty succeeding in their academic studies when competing with peers who had a head start before they arrived at the classroom door.

In their study, Hart and Risley also observed significant differences in the type of feedback and encouragement that students from different socioeconomic backgrounds received from their families. The children in white-collar families heard "encouraging or positive words" an average of 32 times per hour and received only 5 negative comments or directions during that same time period; those in working-class families heard an average of 12 positive and 7 negative comments each hour; and those in low-income families, 5 encouraging comments and a whopping 11 negative comments per hour. The level of motivation and self-esteem of these children would certainly be vastly different!

How Can Vocabulary Gaps Be Minimized?

Although the task is enormous and must begin as early in a child's life as possible, research has proven that vocabulary and knowledge gaps can be minimized for students who have not had optimal language exposure early in their lives (Snow, Barnes, Chandler, Goodman, & Hemphill, 1992). A good example of this is the Carolina Abecedarian Project (Campbell, Pungello, Miller-Johnson, Burchinal, & Ramey, 2001). The data from this 21-year longitudinal study of low-income individuals show that children should be exposed to rich and extensive experiences from infancy through the early school years. Throughout the project, children from low-income backgrounds scored higher on cognitive tests than did their control-group peers. It was also clear that the academic achievement in both reading and math was higher for the study group. In addition to the academic benefits, the study group experienced lifestyle changes: on average, the young people in the treatment group were older when they had their first child and more likely to attend a four-year college than their peers in the control group. Overall, early intervention programs such as the Early Training Project (Gray, Ramsey, & Klaus, 1982) and the High/Scope Perry Preschool Project (Berrueta-Clement, Schweinhart, Barnett, Epstein, & Weikart, 1984) have continued to show success on the academic achievement of high-poverty students (Campbell et al., 2001).

Word Understanding Develops Gradually

Learning the meaning of various words is a continuous, evolving process. As Blachowicz and Fisher (2000) note, understanding the meaning of any word is like flicking on "a light dimmer switch that gradually produces an increasing supply of light" (p. 3) as our experience with the word grows.

There are many levels of word understanding. At the lowest level, we have no knowledge of the word; we do not recognize it and have no idea what it means. At the next level of understanding, we may be able to read the word when we encounter it in context or perhaps even pronounce it in isolation. We may even have a vague sense of having heard the word before, but we can't really say what it means. At the third level, we may have a vague notion of what the word means and perhaps even understand it when used appropriately in conversation, but we can only provide a very vague sense of what it means in the broadest of terms. At the fourth level of understanding, we can provide a general definition of the word and use it in speech or writing. The fifth and highest level of word understanding is when we can define a word precisely, provide synonyms and examples of its use in context, and use it with ease in our day-to-day reading, writing, and conversation.

Understanding builds as one encounters a word multiple times and sees the word used in different situations (Nagy, 1988). This process has important implications for content-area teachers, as common words are often used differently in different subject areas. Moore and colleagues (2003) remind us that we must consider whether students are familiar with a word when we teach it. They write: "As you consider how to teach word meanings, keep in mind the aspects of labels and concepts. If the word to be taught is one for which students already have the appropriate concept and lack only the label, the teaching task is relatively simple. If, as is more common during subject matter study, students lack both the concept and the label, the task is more difficult" (p. 135). For this reason, content-area teachers must help students learn and understand the vocabulary of the discipline they teach and apply the correct label to the new concepts they meet.

Words must be "hooked" onto experiences in our lives. Nagy (1988) tells us that effective vocabulary instruction must include integration and repetition and have meaning in our lives. For middle and high school teachers, this means focusing on expanding a student's word bank in a deliberate and organized manner. Words must be encountered and used over and over again for them to become part of the student's background knowledge.

Ruddell (2001) reminds us that there is a difference between preparing students to understand words in a particular passage to remove comprehension barriers, and in helping students to assimilate those words into their personal long-term vocabularies. Preparing students to read a text does not ensure that the same words will be transferred to long-term memory and personal usage once the assignment is over, because words are learned incrementally through multiple exposures (Stahl, 2003). According to McKeown, Beck, Omanson, and Pope (1985), as many as 4 encounters with a word do not reliably improve reading comprehension skills; 12 exposures, however, do. We must ensure that words surface again and again for our struggling readers, so that the words can grow brighter each time students encounter them.

One of the best ways to expose all students to new and meaningful vocabulary is through extensive reading with a wide variety of texts. Twenty-five to 50 percent of an individual's vocabulary growth comes from incidental learning and by deducing meaning from the context (Anderson & Nagy, 1991; Nagy, 1987). Discussions in the classroom (Stahl & Vancil, 1986) and in the family (Snow, 1991) promote incidental word learning. If students read an average of 3,000 words per day, they will encounter approximately 10,000 new words per year. For children who have a limited vocabulary to begin with, this additional exposure to new words in practical context will have a significant effect. For example, if a 5th grader reads for an hour each day, five days per week, at a conservative rate of only 150 words per minute, the student will read approximately 2,250,000 words in the span of a year. Even if only 2 to 5 percent of the words are new, the student will be exposed to approximately 45,000 to 112,500 new words per year. If the student encounters 5 to 10 percent new words from a single reading, this additional reading exposure would add at least 2,250 new words to the student's vocabulary (Herman, Anderson, Pearson, & Nagy, 1987; Nagy, Anderson, & Herman, 1987; Nagy, Herman, & Anderson, 1985). For a high school student who takes five subjects a day, learning 10 new words every day in each subject would result in as many as 1,800 new words per school year (in addition to those learned from content reading).

By the time good readers reach high school, they possess approximately 1 million words in their four vocabularies, whereas struggling readers may have only 100,000 words (Nagy & Anderson, 1984). Unfortunately, we know that because poor readers often do not have a strong vocabulary, their comprehension also suffers. If a text is filled with unknown words, it will have little meaning for an already reluctant reader. As a result, good readers improve even more, while the gap in word knowledge and background information between the two groups of students widens even further (Stahl, 1999; Stanovich, 1986). As reading expert Louisa Moats (2001) notes, "Older students have experienced reading failure from an early age so they must be convinced that a renewed investment of energy will be worthwhile" (pp. 37–38).

The Components of Vocabulary Knowledge

Identification of the printed word begins with a visual process that concentrates on the forms of the letters in the word. Once the brain initially identifies it, the word is linked to stored knowledge. By examining our prior knowledge of a topic as well as other factors, such as the context, we determine the meaning and even the pronunciation of the word (for example, the word *read* can be pronounced either as "reed" or "red" depending on the meaning of the sentence). Our brains must consider the context and make a split-second decision on how we will interpret a word so that the sentence will make sense; if the wrong decision is made, or we have no frame of reference from which to interpret the word, then comprehension is lost. Good readers have "fix-up" strategies that they apply to the text, such as rereading the passage, while poor readers simply give up on the task altogether.

Another factor behind word comprehension is the breadth of a student's sight word vocabulary. By the end of 1st grade, most children know between 4,000 and 6,000 words (Chall, 1987). Thirteen words—*a, and, for, he, in, is, it, of, that, the, to, was,* and *you*—account for approximately 25 percent of all words found in school texts (Johns & Lenski, 2001), and just 109 words account for half (Kucera & Francis, 1967); about 5,000 words account for nearly 90 percent of the words in elementary school textbooks (Adams, 1990). Ensuring that elementary students can recognize these high-frequency words will enhance reading ability.

Good readers have a vast storehouse of sight words to draw from when reading. Struggling readers or English-language learners will benefit greatly from exposure to sight word lists, such as the Fry and Dolch lists, because the words make up approximately 65 percent of those in the written material students are likely to encounter (Fry, Kress, & Fountoukidis, 1993). However, older students learn words better when they are connected together in meaningful phrases rather than presented as single words (Rasinski, 1990). Teaching in phrases also helps students develop the concept of chunking.

In addition to an individual's sight word knowledge, background knowledge helps determine an individual's familiarity with the terms found in a given text (Nagy & Scott, 2000). As Moats (2001) points out, "Effective vocabulary study occurs daily and involves more than memorizing definitions. Teachers deliberately use new words as often as possible in classroom conversation. They reward students for noticing word usage outside of class. Such strategies as using context to derive meanings, finding root morphemes, mapping word derivations, understanding word origins, and paraphrasing idiomatic or special uses for words are all productive" (pp. 37–38).

Teaching Vocabulary in the Classroom

Helping students expand their vocabularies in all disciplines is vital to promoting vocabulary expansion. An effective vocabulary development program for students in grades 4–12 should include three main strategies:

1. Promoting broad and intensive reading and oral discussions,
2. Encouraging students to experiment with words, and
3. Explicitly teaching word meanings and word-learning strategies.

Beck, Perfetti, and McKeown (1982) describe the most successful classrooms as being "word-aware" places where students practice these strategies regularly. Effective teachers intentionally focus on enriching and expanding students' vocabulary knowledge and model inquisitiveness about words and their meanings; they also help students develop their own skills as independent word learners (Nagy & Scott, 2000). We will look at each of the three instructional strategies and show how you can foster language development on a day-to-day basis.

Promoting Broad and Intensive Reading and Oral Discussions

Students need to be surrounded by oral language and immersed in print. They learn new words when they are read to, when they read extensively themselves, and when conversation and discussion are part of their lives both in school and at home (Snow, 1991). When extensive and stimulating discussions don't occur at home on a regular basis, it is especially vital that school be a place where this does happen.

Students, especially English-language learners and those from low-income homes, need to hear words spoken correctly before they are asked to speak, read, or write them themselves. We must expand our students' vocabularies by fostering rich and descriptive discussions in our classrooms every day. Because many words are not part of students' day-to-day experiences, we must help them discover and understand them. Once students have incorporated new words into their listening vocabularies, we must move the words to their reading, writing, and speaking vocabularies so that they can join the students' regular lexicons.

The best way to learn vocabulary is to connect words to the actual things that they represent—be they experiences, models, or even pictures. Organizing words into graphic picture maps helps students think about relationships and find synonyms for words that connect the words to long-term memory; picture links and memory cues help students to remember the words better.

One strategy for linking oral and written language is to have students keep vocabulary logs or notebooks. As they read, have students jot down interesting words and phrases they find. The logs can be organized alphabetically or by special labels and can include dictionary definitions of words, students' interpretations of them, examples of appropriate use, and pictures of what the words represent. Students can also categorize their words into meaningful groups that make sense to them; examples might include Unusual Words, Colorful Adjectives, Amazing Adverbs, Ugly Words, Words with Pizzazz, Funny Words, and so forth. Ideally, as students become more familiar with the words, they will use them as they write or even in normal day-to-day conversation. Give bonus points to students for successfully incorporating newly learned words into their writing whenever possible.

English words have many connotations that are not readily apparent to non-English speakers. We must help our students discriminate the various uses and shades of meaning associated with each word so that they can understand and use them accurately. These subtle nuances often confuse struggling readers and cause them to lose comprehension.

Multiple Sources

To encourage students to read more, we must provide them with a wide variety of materials on a given topic. These materials should be of various reading levels and should include a wide array of trade books and multiple genres. A single textbook that may well be two years above the class's reading level will not produce the levels of understanding and overall learning growth that teachers want in their students.

Richard Allington (2002) studied what exemplary high school teachers did differently from their less successful peers. According to Allington:

> Exemplary teachers created a multi-sourced and multi-leveled curriculum that did not rely on traditional content-area textbooks. They didn't throw those textbooks out but saw them as just one component of their total set of social studies and science curriculum materials. In state history, for instance, the textbook provided a general organizing framework, but students acquired much of their historical content

from tradebooks of multiple genres. In addition, original source materials, Web-based information, and local historians (professional and amateur) all supported students' study of state history." (p. 18)

A wide range of texts alone will not produce magical results, but it will certainly expand students' exposure to new words—especially if they have already developed some basic decoding and fluency skills.

Looking Up Words

Think back on what you did when you encountered words you did not know while reading in school. Though most of our teachers probably advised us to look up unknown words in the dictionary, I'm sure that few of us actually stopped and did so every time—it's disruptive and time-consuming. As a good reader, you probably used strategies that worked for you most of the time, such as reading to the end of the sentence or paragraph, then checking for understanding. If you got the gist of what was meant, you probably went on reading and ignored the unknown word. If that did not help, you probably stopped to examine the word itself to see if any part of it was recognizable. Were any of the prefixes or root words known to you? If so, perhaps you tried to combine this knowledge with the context to determine the meaning. If this strategy did not help, perhaps you tried to pronounce the word orally to see if it sounded like a word you knew. Perhaps there was a footnote or a definition in a glossary that could help. If none of these strategies worked, most of us probably called upon the knowledge of a parent or teacher who was handy.

Struggling readers have not discovered these strategies for dealing with new words, so teachers should model them. Because students are not likely to reach for the dictionary with every unknown word, teach them how to make reasonable guesses about the word's meaning and then to read on for clarification. Students should know how to consult a reference source, such as a dictionary or a textbook glossary, for assistance when other strategies fail to clarify the meaning. Don't assume that middle or high school students know how to correctly use these tools. Teach them how to use dictionary guide words to locate entries, and how to interpret the entries. Many teachers incorrectly assume that older students have mastered these skills in lower grades.

Students often have difficulty figuring out which definition is correct for the word they are checking. In such cases, have them predict what they think a synonym for the word might be based on the context of the passage. When students have some inkling of what a word might mean before looking it up, they can more readily identify the correct definition. For poor spellers, spelling calculators are available from most discount chain stores for about 10 dollars. Such devices can save struggling readers a lot of frustration, and make good gift ideas for parents.

Studies indicate that active processing of words and manipulation of them in a variety of sensory formats is far superior to the traditional write-the-definition approach to new-word acquisition (Blachowicz & Fisher, 2000). One example would be a Word Wall of interesting words on a classroom bulletin board. Asking students to help compile such a list ensures student ownership and interest in the words selected, and studies indicate that this is a powerful learning tool (Haggard, 1982; Blachowicz, Fisher, Costa, & Pozzi, 1993). Teachers can feature words that fit a certain category or follow a specific pattern, such as "-ology" or "hydro-" words, and might include a section devoted to synonyms for common words. Students should discuss the various words on the Word Wall often, especially if there are many English-language learners in the classroom (Jiminez, 1997). Some additional ideas for word collecting, exposing students to a large number of words, or expanding classroom Word Walls are provided for your consideration.

Unusual-Word Wall

Ask students to post unusual words that they find—the more unusual, the better. Discuss the words with students until they have a good understanding of what they mean and how they are used. Encourage students to provide an illustration of the word or synonyms to go with the posting. You may also choose to create different categories, such as hard-to-pronounce words, words we don't understand, ugly words, or words that are spelled funny.

Word Family Charts

Have students develop charts or posters that show word families or synonym groupings. Ask them to design graphic organizers to show the relationships among the words and how each relates to its synonyms. For example, if the word *walk* is at the center of the chart, it might be surrounded by words organized into categories, such as "words that mean to walk quickly." These charts are especially useful for helping students find more colorful or descriptive words to use in their writing. Another idea is to use as the center of the chart a word that has multiple meanings.

Word Collectors

Have students collect new words they come across and feature them on a "New Words" bulletin board. Ask each contributor to post a word along with a definition and a telling example of the word in use. An illustration can help clarify the meaning for other students. Students should also keep personal dictionaries in a three-ring or spiral notebook, adding new words and examples to it as they encounter them.

Word Banks for Writing

In the primary grades, teachers often provide students with a bank of words on the blackboard to stimulate thinking and writing. Struggling readers often have difficulty getting started writing because no words come to mind when they are asked to do so. To help these students, ask the class to brainstorm some words related to the topic at hand. As the words are provided, write them on the board and leave them for students as a cue while writing. This technique is particularly useful for content writing, where key terms are often very technical.

Opposites

Give students two antonyms, such as *beautiful* and *ugly* or *fat* and *skinny*. Ask them to locate at least five additional words that show the various degrees between the two words (e.g., *beautiful, pretty, attractive, common, plain, unattractive, ugly*). Have students write these words in their journals so they can use them while writing. This activity is helpful for English-language learners, especially if you ask them to discuss the shades of meaning that separate the words and justify the order in which the words are placed.

Share a Word

Charge students with locating one or two words that they think the class should learn. On a specific day, have students bring in their words and take turns discussing where they found them (bringing the example if possible), what they think the words might mean, and why the words are important for the class to know. List the words on the chalkboard as they are presented. When all the students have presented their words, have the class discuss the list and select five to seven words that they would like to emphasize that week, then plan activities that reinforce and clarify the selected words. (The remaining words can be scheduled into other weeks of the quarter.) Place the words of the week on the classroom's Word Wall for reinforcement, and encourage students to use the words whenever possible.

Draw a Word

As new words are reviewed, have students draw pictures to illustrate them. Label each picture so that it is clearly associated with the word it represents. Students will love taking turns creating drawings, but before they start be sure to set ground rules for taste and acceptability.

Bookmark Recorders

Give students their own bookmarks and ask them to jot down interesting or unusual words or phrases on them as they read. Ask them to periodically illustrate some of the words or phrases or otherwise share them with the class. Filled bookmarks can be posted on a special bulletin board for others to read and enjoy.

Another way to use bookmarks is to provide students with a list of key new words, along with a brief definition of each, before they start to read a specific text. As students encounter the new words, they can refresh their memories about what the words mean by checking their bookmarks. Students can jot down any terms that they don't understand or questions about the text on the reverse side of the bookmark. This way the student has a ready reference for classroom discussion of the material.

Word Relationships

Ask students to explore synonyms, antonyms, homonyms, and homophones by featuring these words on the Word Wall. Students can also make charts, graphs, or webs to display the word relationships. Later, they can use the words they identify to create funny stories.

Memory Links

We have probably all used mnemonics or picture images to remember things before, such as the mnemonic "every good boy does fine" for the lines on a musical staff. Developing mnemonics or visual pictures for vocabulary terms is also a good way for students to "hook" particularly hard-to-recall words into their long-term memory.

Vocabulary Tree

Create a "tree" on a bulletin board or chart paper. Have students place a "root" word at the bottom of the tree, and fill the branches with words that stem from the root.

Multiple-Meaning Words

Help students examine the multiple meanings of words by providing them with sentence stems. Students can either draw pictures to illustrate the differences or provide a descriptive sentence. Here are some examples of sentence stems for the word *bank*:

1. What would the word *bank* mean to a person who works in a financial institution?
2. What would the word *bank* mean to a person who navigates a riverboat?
3. What would the word *bank* mean to a pilot flying a plane?
4. What would the word *bank* mean to a little child?

You can also use the "Asking Questions" strategy (Beck & McKeown, 1983) to help explain words. Asking students to explain concepts in a "why" or "why not" format (e.g., "Why would a hermit not enjoy shopping?"). Students like the mystery around such questions, which also have great "hooks" to help them ground the words in their long-term memory banks.

Mood Collages

Ask students to find words that denote certain moods. Cut out pictures that illustrate various moods and display them around the room.

Word Races

Assign groups of students a simple word for which there are many synonyms, and see which group can come up with the most synonyms for its word in a given amount of time.

Semantic Maps

Give students lists of words and categories into which the words fall. Divide the class into groups, and ask them to create semantic maps by placing the words into the appropriate categories in a given amount of time. When they're finished, have the groups discuss their maps and the accuracy of their guesses. Create correct semantic maps and post them in the classroom.

Posting Words

When they read, ask students to post sticky notes on pages that contain unfamiliar words. Ask them to guess from the context or the parts of the word what they think the word may mean before looking up the definition to see how close they are. This technique keeps students reading while at the same time clarifying things that confuse or slow them down.

Words New to Me

Have students find at least four words that they don't know in newspapers or magazines. After they look up the definitions, have them discuss each of the word's meanings and probable usage with at least two friends, then check the groups' conclusions for accuracy. Once each group thoroughly understands all eight words, have the students create a graphic representation of each to place on a special "Words New to Me" bulletin board.

Classifying New Words

Divide students into partners or small groups and give them a list of 15 to 20 words related to a topic you are about to introduce. Ask students to organize the words into three columns—

"know it (can use it or define it)," "heard it but don't know it well," and "never heard it." When they're done, ask them to share their lists and decide how to approach moving words from the second column into the first column.

Word Wall Bingo

Provide students with 6" x 6" grids and ask them to fill in words of their choice from the Word Wall. Read the definitions for the words from slips of paper drawn out of a box. Have students cover the words that match the definition being read until all the spaces in a vertical, horizontal, or diagonal line are covered. Another version of this game can be played with the teacher displaying sentences with one word missing on the overhead projector.

Colorful Phrases

Have students note colorful phrases related to animals that they hear or find while reading (e.g., "Don't make a pig of yourself," "I don't give a hoot"). Post these phrases on the Word Wall for all to enjoy; students can even create stories from them.

Encouraging Students to Experiment with Words

People with large vocabularies tend to be intrigued by words and enjoy playing with them (Beck, McKeown, & Kucan, 2002). One of the goals of effective vocabulary development is to pique student curiosity about words and help them have fun with them. Students should see vocabulary learning as a fun and challenging activity, not drudgery. According to Heath (1983), classrooms should be places where students serve as "language detectives," studying how people talk with different groups and in different situations. Activities that promote wordplay and word consciousness include puns, limericks, riddles, anacrostics, anagrams, crossword puzzles, and even jokes. An outstanding Web resource for older readers for puzzles, word games, thematic vocabulary lists, lesson plans, and help with SAT, ACT, and TOEFL preparation is http://www.vocabulary.com. Two excellent sites for helping English-language learners are http://www.englishclub.com/ and http://www.manythings.org/.

Below are some strategies for helping students have fun with words.

Act It Out

Give students a word and ask them to pantomime (i.e., silently act out) the meaning of the word for the rest of the class. If the student successfully completes the task, the class will have a clear understanding of what the word means and will be able to guess the definition of the word. The tactile representation will be a memory clue for students, in addition to being a fun game.

Be the Author

Ask students to read several picture books, such as *That's Good! That's Bad!* by Margery Cuyler (1991), to observe how authors play with words in their writing. Shel Silverstein's poems are also a good source of creative language. Ask students to create similar imaginative stories or poems using these books as a source of inspiration.

Crossword Puzzle Maker

Ask students to find new words related to a study topic. Using one of many easily available computer-software crossword puzzle makers, have the students design crossword puzzles to exchange with classmates, using key topic terms and newly discovered words. Have contests to see how quickly groups can accurately complete the puzzles.

Illustrated Vocabulary

Have students write words in such a way that they visually display their definition. For example, the word *tall* could be written in large, skinny letters, and the word *short* in squatty, fat letters. Challenge students to be creative in their visual representations and to find unusual words that no one else has illustrated.

Make a New Word

Ask teams of students to take a long word, such as *astonishment*, and see how many words they can make from its letters in an allotted time. While students are having a good time playing around with the word, they will also be picking up new vocabulary as they manipulate and form new words as a team. Students must be able to provide at least a simple definition of each word formed from the longer word in order for it to count, so pick words at random from the list and ask students to define them. This is a particularly good activity for English language-learners, as it will expand the words that they will see and hear.

Fit the Category

Provide students with a long word that contains 10 to 15 letters, such as *Thanksgiving*. Next provide them with a specific category: for example-vegetables, things in the home, countries, or famous people. Working within a time limit, ask small teams of students to think of words that begin with the letters of the given word and also fit the category. The players with the most unique words at the end of the time limit win the round.

Definition Bee

This strategy follows the same format as a spelling bee, only instead of spelling words the students must provide correct definitions for them. Words should begin easy and become more difficult.

Synonyms, Antonyms, and Homonyms

Cut out stories from the newspaper and have students change as many words as possible to synonyms, antonyms, or even homonyms. Ask students to write evaluations of how the changes affected the meaning of the story. The funnier and more creative the story, the better.

Round-Robin Word

Have all students in the class stand. Select a common word such as *said* or *walked* and ask each student to provide a synonym for it. If the student can't think of a word within a short time period (10–15 seconds) or the word has already been given, have him sit down. Continue playing until there is only one person left standing.

Lists and More Lists

Challenge small groups of students to find words in the newspaper and categorize them by five common traits. Give students a specific time limit and see which group can come up with the most categorized words. Students must be able to define all the words and be prepared to tell why the word fits under its category.

Finding Palindromes

Have students work in teams to find as many words as possible that are the same when spelled both forward and backward, such as *deed* or *mom,* or that form new words when spelled backward, such as *drab/bard.* Allow students to use dictionaries to find these words. Anagrams are also fun for students to explore.

Hink-Pinks, Hinky-Pinky, and Hinkety-Pinkety

Have students put their heads together to create fun hink-pink, hinky-pinky, and hinkety-pinkety riddles. These are riddles the answers to which contain an adjective that rhymes with a noun in an amusing way. Hink-pinks contain two one-syllable words that rhyme; hinky-pinkies and hinkety-pinketies contain two two- and three-syllable words that rhyme, respectively. An example of a hinky-pinky would be: "What do you call a rural police officer? A county Mountie."

Word Jeopardy!

Make a Jeopardy!-style game board on the blackboard, complete with dollar categories. Assign student teams to select a category. The "answers" in each category should be definitions, and the students' task is to identify the word being defined in the form of a question (e.g., "What is *simile*?"). The higher the dollar value of the answer chosen, the more difficult the term should be. Students will love playing the game and will clamor to play over and over again.

Which One Doesn't Belong?

Give students a set of four or five words. Ask them to work with a partner or a small group to examine each word and determine which one does not belong and why. Example: In the set *flower*, *pistil*, *organ*, *leaf*, and *stem*, the word *organ* doesn't belong.

Homophone Stories

Read picture books out loud that use homophones in creative ways, such as F. Gwynne's *Chocolate Moose for Dinner* (1976) and *The King Who Rained* (1970). Ask students to create their own homophone stories using as much creativity as possible.

Idioms in the Classroom

Read picture books out loud that feature idiomatic expressions, such as M. Terban's *Mad as a Wet Hen* (1987). Ask students to draw comparisons between the literal and figurative meanings in the book. Have small groups of students work together to create their own books that feature idiomatic expressions.

Password

Divide students into two teams and ask two members from each team to come to the front of the room. Write down a vocabulary word and show it to one student from each team without the other two team members seeing it. Have the students take turns giving their respective team partners a single-word clue about the mystery word until one of the partners guesses the word. The team that figures the word out first gets a point, and four new people come to the front for the next round.

Guess My Word

Place 5 to 10 vocabulary words that are new to students on the board. Create a few descriptive or clarifying clues for each word. Read the clues to the class and have students guess which words match them. Have students think aloud as they explain their choices.

Class Thesaurus

Develop an oversized class thesaurus to which students can add new terms and synonyms as they learn them. Students can use the book to expand their writing and reading activities; in content-area classrooms, students can also make dictionaries with definitions of key terms.

Time's Up!

Ask teams of students to write as many words as they can think of that fit a specific category within a limited time frame. Categories can be broad, such as "sports words," "animal words," "words around the home," "words for things that are green," and so on. Whoever comes up with the most words wins. Bonus points can be given to students who think of words no one else in the class thought of.

Word Games for the Classroom

Purchase Scrabble and Boggle games for the classroom from yard sales around town or ask parents to donate them. Allow students to play the games as a reward for jobs well done. Not only are these games fun and motivating, they also reinforce student vocabulary and reading skills.

Predict the Story

Select key vocabulary words from a text that tell the who, what, where, when, and why of the story. Have students brainstorm how the words are connected and write a paragraph predicting what they think the story is about based on the words. Verify the predictions by reading the whole text to the class and discussing how the words are interrelated.

Alliteration Please

Students can have a good time working in teams to create a book for fellow primary students that contains alliterative sentences from A to Z. Example: On the "A" page of the book, students might write, "All alligators are allowed apples." Onomatopoeic words could be used for an additional touch of creativity, and dictionary use should be encouraged.

Explicitly Teaching Word Meanings and Word-Learning Strategies

Teachers in grades 4–12 introduce students to new terms and ways of using words as they teach their content material. For example, in math, students already know words such as *area*, *mean*, *radical*, *angle*, and *power*. If you ask them to tell you what these words mean, they probably can—but not necessarily in the way that the words are used for content purposes. For example, students might define *area* as a place and *mean* as a synonym for *cruel*. It is imperative that teachers teach how new content-area terms are to be interpreted in class. Help students make a list of words with the "everyday" definition alongside the content-specific one, as in the chart in Figure 3.1. When students link the known with the new, greater learning can result.

Many teachers introduce vocabulary by going over words with students and asking them to copy their definitions. Some teachers even admit that they don't do much to ensure student mastery of content vocabulary because they really have not been trained in reading instruction. They may write terms on the board or ask students to match terms with their definitions, but these approaches seldom result in long-term vocabulary retention; they help students learn the terms they'll be tested on, which they often promptly forget when the class moves on to the next unit.

We know from research that the old teaching method of "assign, define, test" is inadequate for effective vocabulary development in the classroom (Allen, 1999; Baumann & Kameenui, 1991; Beck, McKeown, & Kucan, 2002). Another

Figure 3.1
Content Vocabulary Definition Chart

Term	What It Means to Me	What It Means in Math
area		
mean		
table		
even		
odd		
angle		
rational		

common instructional method is to provide students with lists of words that they have to look up in the dictionary and have them generate sentences using the words. This technique is also largely ineffective, as it does not help students discriminate between the various meanings of the words being studied. When students use dictionary definitions to create sentences, research suggests that 60 percent of the sentences are completely unacceptable (McKeown, 1993). In addition, Scott and Nagy (1989) found that students tend to use only one or two of the listed dictionary definitions for a given word. I am sure we have all had a chuckle over some of the silly or odd sentences that students have written using this approach.

If students are to internalize words and make them permanent additions to their vocabularies, they must be given time to understand the words and become familiar with all aspects of them. Give students synonyms, examples, and nonexamples of appropriate usage whenever possible so that they can thoroughly understand how particular words are applied. Older students need to more deeply explore words in order to really incorporate them into their growing vocabularies (Beck, McKeown, & Kucan, 2002). Because there are so many words that our students need to learn over the course of their schooling, we cannot leave vocabulary development to chance.

Certain words are needed simply to help students process a text, but not for long-term vocabulary. Teachers should explicitly teach these words during the prereading process, but as an aid to comprehension and little more. The words *photosynthesis* and *mitosis* are good examples of such terms: if an entire unit will be about learning to understand the concepts these words represent, it would be impractical for students to learn more than an introductory definition at the beginning of the unit. As instruction continues, the concepts behind the term will become more developed.

To be effective, explicit instruction should not only consist of learning definitions and contextual usage, but also actively involve students in the learning process by relating the word to prior knowledge and other words in the students' word banks. It is only when solid links are made in the brain that these words will become a part of the accessible vocabulary.

Other words that should be explicitly taught include those that

- Students are likely to encounter again and again in the material being studied,
- Have multiple meanings,
- Have multiple pronunciations (e.g., *bow*),
- Are easily confused (e.g., *accept* and *except*), and
- Are pronounced the same but spelled differently (e.g., *their, they're,* and *there*).

Older students should also be explicitly taught prefixes, suffixes, and root words. Brown and Cazden (1965) indicate that approximately 30 root words, prefixes, and suffixes provide the basis for more than 14,000 commonly used words in the English language:

1. *ab* (away from)
2. *ad* (to, toward)
3. *co, con, com, col, cor* (together, with)
4. *de* (away, down, out of)
5. *dis* (not, opposite)
6. *ex* (out of, formerly)
7. *in, im, il, ir* (in, not)
8. *pre* (before)
9. *pro* (forward)
10. *re* (back, again)
11. *un* (not, opposite)
12. *able* (capable of, worthy of)
13. *ance, ence, ancy, ency* (act or fact of doing, state, quality)
14. *er, or* (person or thing connected with, agent)
15. *ful* (full of, abounding in)
16. *less* (without, free from)

17. *ly* (like, characteristic of)
18. *ment* (state of, quality of)
19. *tion, sion, xion* (action, state, result)
20. *phon* (sound, speech)
21. *tele* (distance)
22. *meter* (measure)
23. *cap* (to seize, take, or contain)
24. *audio* (to hear)
25. *vid, vis* (to see or look at)
26. *spect* (to observe, watch)
27. *inter* (between)
28. *sub* (under)
29. *mis* (wrong)
30. *trans* (across or beyond)

Several Latin verbs will also assist students in deciphering word meanings. They are as follows:

■ *Tenere* (to have, hold) as in *tenable, tenacious,* and *tenant*;
■ *Mittere* (to send, launch) as in *message, missile,* and *missive*;
■ *Facere* (to do, make) as in *faction, artifact,* and *manufacture*; and
■ *Scribere* (to write) as in *scribble, scribe, and script.*

Lengthy words can be overwhelming. The following list of Latin roots might help students to unlock the meaning of such words more quickly:

■ *aud* (to hear)
■ *dict* (to speak or tell)
■ *min* (small)
■ *mit, mis* (to send)
■ *ped* (foot)
■ *port* (carry)

- *scrib, script* (write)
- *spect* (see)
- *struct* (build, form)

Some common Greek roots that might be helpful include:

- *astro* (star)
- *bio* (life)
- *geo* (earth)
- *meter* (measure)
- *phon* (sound)

Content-area teachers should also prepare lists of common word parts specific to the subject being taught. One Web site that you might find helpful for teaching prefixes and suffixes is http://www.wordexplorations.com.

Providing a word's "history" can help make some words more memorable for students. For example, knowing that "mort" comes from the French word for death will help students unlock the meaning of *mortuary*, *immortal*, or *mortal*. Model thinking aloud about how word parts can unlock meaning, so that students have the skill in their bag of reading tricks.

Here are some strategies to help students learn about word parts.

Cloze Passage

Place students in groups of two or three. Provide each group with a paragraph where blanks are strategically substituted for key vocabulary terms. Provide students with a list of words (preferably with a few more words than fit into the paragraph) and a dictionary. Allow students to look up the vocabulary words and then, as a group, to discuss where each term might fit into the paragraph. When all students have completed the task, display the completed paragraph with the missing terms on the overhead. Discuss any discrepancies. Point out why certain words won't fit a given sentence, but feel free to approve "creative" choices that fit even if they're not the intended words.

Using Prefixes

Ask students to work in teams to generate a list of words with prefixes. Have them explain how they know the difference between words with actual prefixes and words that simply start with the same letters.

Mapping a Word Core

Give students a word part and ask them to work together to build a semantic web around it. For example, if the word part is *photo*, students could link it to such words as *photosynthesis*, *photograph,* and *telephoto.* Seeing how words interconnect will make the word part more meaningful and memorable to the students.

Graphic Organizers

Graphic organizers can help students pictorially link words with their synonyms. Have students create illustrations that help convey the meanings of words, and ask them to write definitions in their own terms. You might also ask them to write out scenarios for each word by answering questions, such as "Describe a time when your parents admonished you for something you did," "Tell about a time when someone around you acted conceited," or "What would you do if you were a philatelist?"

You Guessed It

Once students have learned to deconstruct words into parts, give pairs of students a group of words and ask them to predict their meaning by conducting detective work. Most students will like the challenge of working together and playing detective. After they've worked with the words for a while, provide students with the words used in an appropriate sentence. See if this new information changes their predictions in any way. Ask students to pretend that they work for a dictionary company and have to create entries for these words. Once they've done so, have them compare their work to the actual dictionary definition. How close were they on each word? Which definition is easier to understand and remember?

Shades of Meaning

Give students groups of related words (e.g., *overweight*, *plump*, *fat*, and *obese*). Ask them to discuss the connotations and nuances of each, and have them order the words from nicest to harshest, providing a rationale for their decisions.

Dictionary Collections

Work with students to create classroom dictionaries of synonyms, antonyms, homonyms, and idioms. Make sure that definitions are written in students' own words rather than copied out of published dictionaries. If possible, each entry should contain a picture as well as some sample sentences showing proper usage of the word. Dictionaries can even be kept from year to year, with each class adding their entries in a different color. Each subsequent class could be challenged to see if it can add more pages to the dictionary than the previous classes.

Etymology Lessons

Many outstanding resource books describe the history behind various words. Have students research the history of several new words and present this information to the class. The stories will help students remember the new word, and may even build curiosity about how other words came to be as well.

Sorting Words and Finding Links

Ask students to categorize given content words and explain their decisions afterward. For example, if the class is studying weather terms, words for categorization may include *hurricane, windy, sunny, cirrus, stratus, flood, rainy, earthquake, cumulus, blizzard, nimbostratus,* and *humid.*

Concept Map

Have students classify new words by filling in the blanks in a concept map (see Figure 3.2 for an example).

Figure 3.2
Sample Concept Map

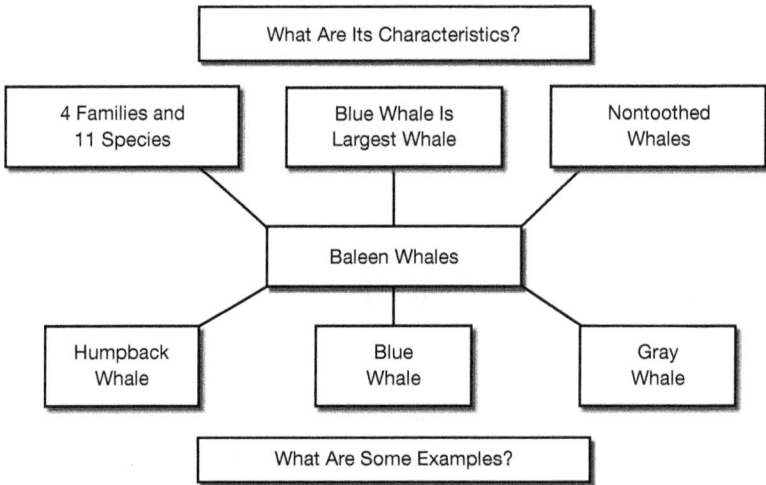

| What Are Its Characteristics? |
| 4 Families and 11 Species | Blue Whale Is Largest Whale | Nontoothed Whales |
| Baleen Whales |
| Humpback Whale | Blue Whale | Gray Whale |
| What Are Some Examples? |

Frayer Vocabulary Model

Originally developed by Frayer, Frederick, and Klausmeier (1969), the Frayer vocabulary model is a helpful, time-tested way for students to learn new words more deeply. For every word, the Frayer model asks students to write down a definition and lists of characteristics, examples, and nonexamples (see Figure 3.3 for an example).

Figure 3.3
Frayer Vocabulary Model for the Word *Rectangle*

Definition (In Your Own Words)	Important Characteristics
A box with two sets of equal and parallel sides.	• Four sides—two sides equal • Parallel lines with four right angles • Opposite sides parallel; four lines of symmetry

Rectangle

Examples	Nonexamples
• A dollar bill • A poster • A wagon • Notebook paper	• A coin • A ball • A wheel

Foreign Contributions

Ask students to make lists of words classified by country of origin, then to compare and contrast how close the word's English meaning is to the meaning in the original language. Lists of "borrowed" words can be posted on bulletin boards around the classroom for others to explore as well.

Be the Teacher

Give pairs of students a list of 10 to 15 new words. Ask each pair to examine the words and thoroughly discuss the meanings of any words that they know. Have the students write short, original definitions for each of the known words and provide an example of how the word might be used in conversation. If one person doesn't know a word that the other person knows, then the knowledgeable student should explain the word to his or her partner. After discussing all the words, the pair should take its definitions list to the teacher for approval, then join up with another pair to see if there are any additional words that they can learn. Again, students should teach each other the meanings of words that they don't understand. The students then add these definitions to their own lists, and the pairs meet with yet another pair to repeat the process. This continues until the teacher calls time or all of the students have obtained definitions for all of the words on the lists. When time is called, students should share their definitions and important understandings about each word with the class.

Spice It Up

Provide students with basic paragraphs that are written in simple, basic sentences. Ask students to rewrite the paragraph by trying to "spice up" the simple vocabulary into more descriptive vocabulary. Students can also take a simple fairy tale, such as "Goldilocks and the Three Bears," and rewrite it using more sophisticated vocabulary. Challenge students to see who can create the most unusual versions of the paragraphs or stories.

What Does It Say?

Teach students how to use the pronunciation guides in dictionaries, so that they can pronounce the words they investigate. Teach them how to interpret the pronunciation symbols and practice reading new words. Have them write words they know using the pronunciation symbols, and practice reading difficult sentences written in the symbols. Students will enjoy the laughs while learning a very valuable skill.

Concept Ladder

A concept ladder (Gillet & Temple, 1996) is a helpful way of asking questions to create a solid definition for a word. The student lists answers to the following questions to demonstrate word meaning through categories, distinguishing features, and examples:

- What is it a kind of? What are kinds of it?
- What is it a part of? What are parts of it?
- What is it a stage or type of? What are stages or types of it?
- What is it a product or result of? What are the products or results of it?

A concept ladder for the word *burrito* might look like this:

- What is it a kind of? food
- What are the parts of it? tortilla, meat, beans, cheese, salsa
- What are stages of it? plain, covered with sauce and cheese, deep fried
- What is it a product of? Frequently eaten in Mexican restaurants or by families who enjoy Mexican food. Available at Taco Bell.

List-Group-Label

This strategy developed by Taba (1967) can be helpful for any content area where students must learn a large number of vocabulary words and how they interrelate. Ask students to generate a list of all the terms they associate with a given word. For example, if the given word is *space*, students might come up with the words *solar system*, *galaxy*, *planet*, *nova*, *dwarf star*, and *black hole*. After all of the words have been listed, ask students to group their words according to a common feature and then label each category. Students must provide a rationale for why each term belongs under the label it has been assigned. Once the words have been categorized, students can create a semantic web to show how the words interrelate. Adding illustrations to the maps can enhance the likelihood that students will commit the words to long-term memory.

Context Clues

One effective strategy to unlock word meanings is to use context clues in sentences and paragraphs. Students should first consider the word on its own, looking for identifiable prefixes, suffixes, or root words that might shed light on the word's meaning. If this is not enough to figure out the meaning of the word in context, the reader should next examine the rest of the sentence for clues. Is there a synonym that would make sense if substituted for the word in question? If not, then the reader should consider the topic of the paragraph. What meaning might make sense in light of the content of the passage?

If all of these strategies fail to produce a viable suggestion for the meaning of the unknown word, then readers must seek assistance from classmates or a dictionary. Demonstrate for students by thinking aloud how one strategy might work better than another for a specific passage. Ask students to also think aloud as they work through paragraphs on their own to clarify meaning.

Signal Word Detective

Help students identify "signal words" in context that may help them find possible contextual hints for new words. When students guess a meaning, have them model out loud their thinking process so that others can hear how they made the deduction.

Guess My Word

At the start of the day, write up to five new words on the chalkboard. Use the words in as many ways as possible in class. Ask students to consider the context of the words and guess what they think the words might mean (no dictionaries allowed). By the end of the class period, see how close students can come to the correct definition of the given words.

Highlighting New Words

Give students sticky notes, which they should place next to any new words they come across while reading. Ask students to use context clues to arrive at a definition of each new word. At the end of the reading session, have students compare notes and check their predictions. As they do this, walk around the room and help correct any misunderstandings. Next, the students should enter their new words into a new-word log, along with a definition in their own words that has been approved by the teacher and a copy of the original sentence in which the word was found.

Building Sentences

Give students lists of words and ask them to create sentences that clearly show the definition of each word. For example, instead of, "There was a lot of debris in the yard," a student might write, "When the bear tipped over the trash can, debris spilled all over the yard." To further scaffold readers, consider providing sentence stems (e.g., "When Mom saw the debris from the trash can all over the yard, she . . .").

Build a Story

Give students a group of words, allowing them to locate the definitions and discuss their various connotations. Ask each student to write a paragraph using as many of the new words as possible. Then ask them to read their paragraphs out loud to see if the group agrees that all of the words are properly used in context. Have students provide feedback and corrections to their group members so that the stories are all correctly written and all words correctly applied.

Yea or Nay?

Read or show students sentences with new words clearly featured. Have students vote "yea" or "nay" on whether the word was appropriately used in the sentence. If the word was not used appropriately, ask for words that could be correctly used in the sentence (Beck & McKeown, 1983). Example: Would an undertaker be buying a gift for his customer?

Word Meanings Web

Give students a word that has multiple meanings and have them create a word meanings web that contains short definitions or synonyms for each word meaning (see Figure 3.4). Students can add illustrations to these charts to make them more interesting and memorable.

Figure 3.4
Word Meanings Web

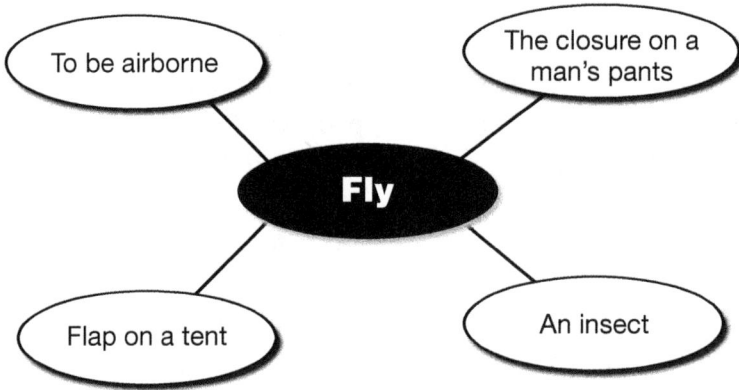

Word Watcher

Word Watcher (also known as Word Wizard) is a technique developed by Beck, McKeown, and Kucan (2002) to help students observe outside the classroom words they've learned in class. Create a chart with each student's name on it and a spot for tally marks. Students can receive a tally either for reporting sightings of target words or for using the words correctly themselves. To earn the point, students must describe the context in which the word was used or heard.

Another idea is to have students watch TV newscasts and find all of the ways that their vocabulary words might apply to one of the news stories presented. Beck, McKeown, and Kucan found that even when "sighting reports" clearly appeared to be fabrications on the part of the student, substantial vocabulary learning was still taking place. The moral of the story is that it's okay to be liberal in awarding points and not worry about whether the "sightings" are real or only imagined. In either case, students are connecting to the vocabulary.

Word Relationship Web

When you want students to learn the various meanings of a word, word relationship webs can help. Begin with a central concept and then help students design a web of meaning relationships that go along with it (see Figure 3.5).

Figure 3.5
Word Relationship Web

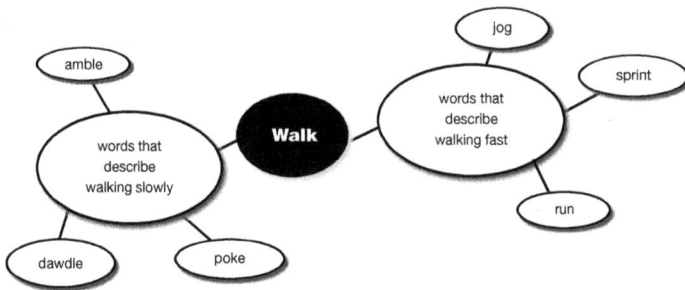

Fill In the Blank

Give students a sheet of text with blanks where key words you want to focus on have been removed. Place the key words either at the bottom of the sheet or on another piece of paper. Have the students read the passage in pairs and determine where each of the missing words would likely fit. With this technique, students also have to examine the grammar and syntax of the sentence. When students are finished, have them discuss the clues that helped them determine where each word should be placed. For particularly low-performing readers, the teacher could even give a synonym or word category hint for each missing word.

Vocabulary Anchoring Chart

As students read, ask them to keep a notebook where they record key features about new words they encounter (see Figure 3.6 for a sample).

Figure 3.6
Vocabulary Anchoring Chart

Unknown Word	Source and Page Where New Word Was Found	What I Infer This Word Might Mean	Actual Definition As Used in This Sentence From a Reference Source	Ways to Remember: A Picture or a Connection I Have Made

Vocabulary Log

Another form of notebook for recording new words is the vocabulary log shown in Figure 3.7.

Writing to Expand Vocabulary

Give students a descriptive word such as *misanthrope* or *alienated*, and ask them to write about someone they know who fits the category, or a time when something happened that could be labeled in this manner. Such connections will help keep the new word stored in the students' long-term memory banks.

Figure 3.7
Vocabulary Log

Sentence with New Word and Page Number	What I Predict the Word Means	The Dictionary Definition of the Word As Used in This Sentence	My Own Sentence with the New Word Used in the Same Context	Picture or Connection for the New Word to Help Me Remember It

Conclusion

Although there are many ways to present vocabulary to students, we know that the most effective techniques help students make connections by examining context, prior background knowledge, and the concepts behind the words (Stahl, 1999). Because vocabulary is fundamental to reading success, we must find ways to interest students in playing with language, expanding their vocabularies and knowledge bases, and engaging in wide reading. We cannot allow huge gaps in vocabulary knowledge to continue to exist between top performers and struggling students, and we must find ways to strengthen and expand the vocabulary sets of all students no matter what their socioeconomic or ethnic backgrounds. All teachers, no matter what content area they teach, must actively engage students in expanding their vocabularies and strategically tackling new words in any text that they are given. When students can do this, they will have the foundation necessary to move to higher levels of literacy.

4 | Comprehension

Comprehension is drawing meaning from words; it is the "essence of reading" (Durkin, 1993), central both to academic and lifelong learning. According to the Rand Corporation, reading comprehension is "the process of simultaneously extracting and constructing meaning through interaction and involvement with written language. It consists of three elements: the reader, the text, and the activity or purpose for reading" (Snow, 2002, p. xii).

Comprehension is a process, not a product. Readers filter understanding through the lens of their motivation, knowledge, cognitive abilities, and experiences. Effective readers have a purpose for reading, and use their background knowledge and experiences to relate to the text: We don't comprehend unless we draw connections between what we read and our background knowledge. Words have to be processed at the "thinking" level before comprehension can take place.

The following four important factors influence reading comprehension:

- Command of the linguistic structure of the text,

- Adequate vocabulary in the content area,

- Degree of metacognitive control of the text, and

- Adequate domain knowledge.

Command of the Linguistic Structure of the Text

Readers need to know how to decode text quickly and easily so that cognitive energy is not drained from the task of drawing meaning from the text. When readers are familiar with the genre and style in which the text is written, they are better able to comprehend the text. For example, most children know that fairy tales begin with the opening, "Once upon a time" and end with the words "The End." Knowing such characteristics helps the reader to anticipate what will come next in the text.

Adequate Vocabulary in the Content Area

A good vocabulary enables readers to process words automatically while reading. Because we can hold no more than seven items in short-term memory at any one time, readers must decode words rapidly (Sousa, 1995). If it takes too long for words to go from short-term memory to being processed at deeper levels, then the words are soon forgotten and no meaning is derived. When a reader stops frequently to determine the meaning of a word or how it fits into the context of the passage, comprehension suffers.

Degree of Metacognitive Control of the Text

Readers must know how to self-monitor and reflect on their level of understanding during the act of reading. They must be able to "listen to" what the words say while they read, monitor comprehension so that they know when it has been lost, and have fix-up strategies ready for use when necessary. Many struggling readers simply give up when they don't understand the text because they don't have strategies in place.

Adequate Domain Knowledge

Background knowledge helps us connect to the text we are reading. Without the ability to connect and relate to the text, we will derive little meaning from it; without meaning, no comprehension can result. When we read, we read *about* something, so our background content knowledge makes a difference in how well we understand the material. Those who possess extensive knowledge on a topic prior to reading about it are able to understand and recall more of the important information from a text than can those with less knowledge (Beck & McKeown, 1998). When students do not have the appropriate background knowledge, teachers must take time to provide experiences or help establish background information prior to asking students to process text.

As Hirsch (2003) notes, it would be a mistake to assume that comprehension problems are limited to disadvantaged children. Hirsch points to three research-based principles for teaching comprehension:

■ Solid fluency skills allow the mind to concentrate on making sense of what we read,

■ Broadening vocabulary increases comprehension and helps further learning, and

■ Possessing a wide background in domain knowledge increases fluency skills, further expands vocabulary, and enables the learner to process text at deeper levels of understanding.

Students must be taught how to comprehend the materials that are presented to them; this ability is not innate. Reading expert Martha Rapp Ruddell (2001) tells us, "In the past, much of the comprehension 'instruction' in secondary schools was little more than teachers *telling* students to read and understand. . . . This approach today seems more than a little short-sighted, especially when viewed in light of the heavy expectations we hold for student learning and development of literacy skills and abilities. Simply *telling* students to read and understand assumes students will be able to do all that we expect them to do without our help. Further, it equates *telling* someone to do something with *teaching* him or her how to do it, and such an equation is simply not valid" (p. 84).

According to Meltzer, Smith, and Clark (2001), some strategies that should be directly taught to all students include

- Rehearsing (underlining and taking notes),
- Elaborating (taking notes by paraphrasing text, forming a mental image, creating an analogy, and summarizing),
- Organizing (outlining and mapping), and
- Comprehension monitoring (metacognitive training and self-questioning skills).

For struggling readers, Meltzer, Smith, and Clark say that the skills of monitoring comprehension and self-questioning while reading must also be taught. To help students learn to process text at high levels, we must think aloud to show them how we apply our own thinking strategies, how to break the text down into manageable units that make sense, and what to do when they lose comprehension.

To increase content knowledge, students must learn how words they already know are used in the content area. According to Searls and Klesius (1984), there are at least 99 common words in English with four or more different definitions or applications. Take the word *stage,* for example. A student in science class may hear his teacher say, "Place the slide on the 'stage' of the microscope and focus the viewfinder." On another day, the same teacher might introduce the idea of the "stages" of metamorphosis, or discuss the "stage" on a rocket ship. If the student then goes to art class, he may hear the teacher discuss doing a clay project in "stages." Later in the week, the student may hear his language arts teacher say that he wants to "set the stage" for a book they are about to begin reading. When the student goes home, perhaps he hears his mother tell his father that her women's group is about to "stage" a fundraiser. Later that evening, watching the TV news, he may hear about a critical situation in which a river is at flood "stage." It's no wonder students are confused about word meaning! We continue to expand our knowledge of words and their various meanings as we encounter them in our daily lives, and we must help students do the same as they work with us in the content areas.

High Background Knowledge Increases Comprehension

Researchers Voss, Vesonder, and Spilich (1980) studied the connection between background knowledge and text understanding by analyzing the comprehension of adults with a high or low initial knowledge of baseball. Subjects read a passage about a baseball game and were then asked to recall what they learned. Individuals from the high-knowledge group not only recalled more of the information, but were also more likely to remember information of greater significance to the game of baseball. Low-knowledge readers, on the other hand, were more likely to remember less significant details, such as the weather, rather than the more significant details about the game itself. Pearson, Hansen, and Gordon (1979) reinforced this observation in a similar study with two groups of 2nd grade students where the differing variable was their background knowledge of spiders. When asked to read and discuss a passage on spiders, the high-knowledge children were better able to answer implicit questions based on the text than their low-knowledge peers. If we want our students to understand and be able to process content material accurately and with good comprehension, we must take the time to help them activate the knowledge they have in each topic prior to continuing the instructional process.

As Hirsch (2003) tells us, "Experiments have shown that when someone comprehends a text, background knowledge is typically integrated with the literal word meanings of the text to construct a coherent model of the whole situation implied by the text. An expert can quickly make multiple connections from the words to construct a situation model. But a novice will have less relevant knowledge and less well-structured knowledge, and will therefore take more time to construct a situation model" (p. 16). This finding reinforces the importance of making sure that students have adequate background knowledge in a topic prior to asking them to read new material.

Building Comprehension Skills

Students must understand that reading *is* thinking. From 4th grade on, most of our work in literacy development is about helping students understand that thinking and making meaning are the essence of reading. To develop this understanding, there are two sets of skills students must have. One set is metacognitive in nature, while the other is composed of skill-based techniques that allow readers to understand the mechanics and organization of reading. While the metacognitive skills allow students to link their thoughts and understandings to prior information in their brains, mechanical skills allow readers to frame their expectations regarding the text and its organization.

When teaching literacy strategies, our goal should be to model them enough that students will learn to use them automatically as they read. As adult readers, we know what to do when material is difficult or our minds wander while reading. When most successful readers realize that they have lost comprehension, they stop reading, go back to the start of where meaning was lost, and reread the passage at a slower rate. They then check again for understanding. Poor readers, on the other hand, do not understand that they should take any action when comprehension is lost.

The brain likes patterns and seeks to connect new learning to prior knowledge and experiences, so it makes sense to provide it with as many ways as possible to connect new information to known information as we are reading. The more ways that knowledge is grounded and secured with links within our mental storehouse, the more accessible and usable the information becomes.

Metacognition can be defined as "thinking about thinking." It involves being aware of and reflecting on our own learning, monitoring our level of understanding, drawing conclusions, and making judgments. We use metacognitive strategies when we want to plan our learning and get over roadblocks that have stopped us from proceeding smoothly. In far too many classrooms, students are passive participants in the learning process; they are not actively engaged in "doing" reading and writing and thinking about their own thinking. As Blachowicz and Fisher (2000) advise, "The idea is to support students by calling on them to survey the selection, activate prior knowledge, make predictions, gather data from reading, make inferences, and monitor their understanding to refine or change their predictions as they go forward, respond to, and use new information. This process is cyclical and takes place repeatedly during reading" (p. 41).

Prediction

One of the first metacognitive skills we use when we read is prediction. From the moment we pick up a book, we begin using our prediction skills. We look at the title of the book, see the picture on the front cover, read the blurb on the back, or notice that our favorite author has written the book. From these first moments, we begin making predictions as to the content, our level of interest, and our desire to read the book. Similarly, when we thumb through a magazine or newspaper, we look at the pictures, headlines, and captions and make a split-second evaluation about whether we will read the article. We anticipate how the book or article might add to our knowledge base, amuse us, or provide information that we might need in the future. When we decide to read a particular text, it is because we have established a "purpose" for doing so. The purpose may be to learn how to do something, to understand a new idea or concept, to update ourselves on a specific set of facts, or simply to enjoy an interesting story. We "anticipate" that we may learn certain concepts, become informed about certain facts or situations, or be moved to experience events vicariously and share emotions. Predicting and anticipating are two vital thinking strategies that we use prior to reading a specific text.

Many students do not have any understanding of how to use predicting or anticipating skills when they read. Their idea of selecting a book is finding the thinnest, least demanding one on the shelf, or the one with the most pictures and the least text. The idea of selecting something that matches their interests, prior knowledge, background, or reading abilities may not occur to them. Talking about our own thinking processes can help our students understand the importance of these criteria, as can asking them to talk about their own thinking processes.

Activating Background Knowledge

Researchers have clearly identified background knowledge as one of the key links to good comprehension and effective learning (Pearson, Hansen, & Gordon, 1979; Voss, Vesonder, & Spilich, 1980). Before beginning any reading assignment, set the stage for students by helping them recall some of what they already know about the topic at hand. Making this connection piques interest and motivates students to read the text. Here are some examples of ways to get students to activate prior knowledge:

■ "Yesterday, we discussed the process of mitosis and read about this process in our textbook. Work with two other people and make a chart that shows as much as you can remember about this process from our discussion yesterday.

As we read today, we will be adding to the information and expanding our knowledge about this topic."

■ "We have all had disappointments happen in our life, and we are going to read about a girl who had to face a great disappointment in her life. Discuss with your small group a big disappointment that you had in your life and how you coped with it."

■ "If you were going to run for president of the United States, make a list of the information you would need to know to run for that office."

Beginning the lesson by asking students to recall what they already know about the topic helps them relate to and connect with the material on a more meaningful and personal level.

As adult readers, we always have a purpose for reading a particular text, even if it's simply enjoyment. We should clarify to students why they will be reading before they read. Is the reading for personal enjoyment, or will the information be used to answer specific questions? Will students be expected to complete a graphic organizer using the new material, or write a summary of key points? Will they be writing a story based on the pattern of the text? Students need to understand how to judge the depth of attention necessary for the task. If students are reading a novel for pleasure, do they understand that the material can be read quickly, without outlining details or taking notes on the material? If they will be asked to construct a summary of the material or take a test on the content, do they understand that more careful reading (including highlighting or note taking) might be in order? If the intent is for students to model their own writing after a specific book, do the students understand that they should pay attention to pattern and detail?

Prereading Strategies

During the prereading phase, we want to ensure that students are introduced to new vocabulary or other unusual features about the text. According to reading expert Kylene Beers (2003), "The more we frontload students' knowledge of a text and help them become actively involved in constructing meaning prior to reading, the more engaged they are likely to be as they read the text" (p. 101). Helping students set a purpose, make connections, and eliminate vocabulary issues improves motivation and promotes more thorough comprehension.

Teachers in content areas should think about what reading skills might help students learn their content. For example, I often hear math teachers complain that students have trouble with word problems, because they struggle with distinguishing relevant information from irrelevant information. One solution is to give students several solutions for a math problem and then ask them to determine which best fits the problem and why. Teachers can also ask student teams to read the math problem and write a "gist" statement in 12 words or less. Students can also mark out all irrelevant information so that they can better understand the information that they will need. Help students with their thinking processes by asking them to write down the steps they used to solve an equation; reading these will help you to isolate any problems or misunderstandings the students may be having. According to Moore and colleagues (2003), math teachers should teach important math prefixes to students, such as the following:

- *bi* (two). Example: *bisect*
- *cent* (hundred). Example: *centimeter*
- *circu* (around). Example: *circle*
- *co, con* (with). Example: *coefficient*
- *dec* (ten). Example: *decimal*
- *dia* (through). Example: *diameter*
- *equi* (equal). Example: *equilateral*
- *inter* (between). Example: *intersect*
- *kilo* (thousand). Example: *kilometer*

- *milli* (thousand). Example: *milligram*
- *peri* (around). Example: *perimeter*
- *poly* (many). Example: *polygon*
- *quadr* (four). Example: *quadrant*
- *tri* (three). Example: *triangle*

Signs around the room with key terms and formulas will also help students improve their math comprehension.

Science and social studies teachers can help students improve their comprehension by using anticipation guides, K-W-L charts, and graphic organizers. Frequently, science and social studies textbooks are organized around a cause-and-effect or time-line format; helping students understand these patterns will increase their ability to process content text. Students also need to understand that textbooks in these content areas are not necessarily read from front to back, and that the material is organized in segments that include subtopics within each chapter. Helping students understand how to read graphs, charts, glossaries, and the insets usually found in textbooks will also help them read more effectively.

The goal of all prereading strategies is to build background knowledge, make connections between old and new knowledge, introduce new vocabulary, preview or examine the text in detail, generate interest in reading the text, make predictions, and help readers set a clear goal and purpose for reading. Such activities, examples of which appear below, motivate students to interact with the text and focus their reading.

Probable Passage

The Probable Passage strategy (Wood, 1984) is a way to help students make predictions about reading content, and can be used with either narrative or expository text. Begin by choosing several vocabulary words from the text that are key to the story or topic or need additional emphasis as new vocabulary words.

Introduce the words to the students and discuss them to clarify their meaning. Next, ask students to develop a paragraph that uses all of the words and predicts what they think the gist of the text will be. After reading, have students verify how close they were in their predictions.

Anticipation Guide

The Anticipation Guide is an effective strategy for helping students raise interest and connect with background knowledge (Heber & Nelson, 1986; Readence, Bean, & Baldwin, 1989). Though useful for narrative text, this strategy is particularly helpful with content-area expository text.

Select 10 to 15 statements (fewer for younger students) or ideas from the text that you think can both help you assess background knowledge and interest students in reading the material, and have students write the statements in their guides. An example of a statement from a narrative text might be, "Older siblings have a responsibility to their younger brothers and sisters." In this case, students might be reading a story in which an older sibling has to save younger brothers and sisters from a crisis situation at some personal cost. An example of a statement from an expository text might be, "Butterflies are the only insects to develop in cocoons." There should be columns marked "True or False" on either side of the statements—one that the students will complete before reading the text, and one for completing afterward. Ask students to examine each statement and determine from their own background knowledge if it is true or false.

After students have done their own predictions, ask them to share them with one another. When students are validating their predictions, have them place sticky notes on the pages where the relevant information can be found. See Figure 4.1 for an example of an Anticipation Guide.

Figure 4.1
Sample Anticipation Guide

Arizona

T		F
_____	1. Arizona gets its name from the Indian word "Arizonac," which means "small spring."	_____
_____	2. Navajos lived in tepees that could be moved easily to follow the herds.	_____
_____	3. Vasquez de Coronado was believed to be the first white man to reach Arizona.	_____
_____	4. The Arizona state tree is the Palo Verde tree.	_____
_____	5. Arizona's state bird is the roadrunner.	_____
_____	6. At 12,633 feet, Mt. Humphreys is Arizona's highest peak.	_____

K-W-L and K-W-W-L Charts

The K-W-L Chart (Ogle, 1986) has been a very popular way for teachers to help students link background knowledge, purpose, and summarization in an effective way. This technique is excellent for beginning units of study where students will be gathering information over a multilesson time frame. Before reading, give students an outline divided into three sections: "Know," "Want to Know," and "Learned." In the "Know" column, have students list what they already know about the topic. In the "Want to Know" column, have students list what they want to learn about the topic. These two columns are completed prior to beginning the unit and reading new text. Some teachers find that asking students to generate lists in small groups rather than as an entire class helps students develop more effective questions for the "Want to Know" column.

After reading the text and completing the unit of study, ask students to complete the third column of the chart by filling in what they have learned during the lesson. If students have conducted multisource research, the addition of a fourth column labeled "Where I Can Find This Info" may be helpful (see Figure 4.2 for an example of a K-W-W-L chart). In this column, students list different sources they think might be worth consulting for answers. The use of multiple sources motivates students and increases student interest.

The K-W-L Chart is most effective when it is used for a large unit of study where the students will be spending some time rather than for a single lesson.

Figure 4.2
Sample K-W-W-L Chart

Know	Want to Know	Where I Can Find This Info	Learned

Prediction Chart

Before reading a section of text, ask students to examine the section headers and captions to predict what they will learn from the material. You can prompt the students with sentence stems: "From the title of this section, I predict this section will tell us. . . ." After reading, match the predictions with the content that was actually learned. How many predictions were accurate? Were there any incorrect assumptions? Students should write their predictions on the left side of a piece of paper and then write statements from the text after reading on the right side for comparison purposes (see Figure 4.3).

Figure 4.3
Predicting Content

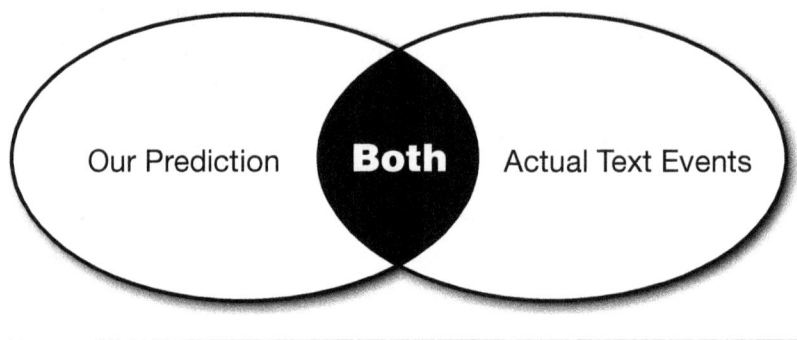

Our Prediction — **Both** — Actual Text Events

Graphic Organizers

Language arts teachers know that story frames or story maps are excellent postreading techniques to help students identify key aspects of a story, such as characters, setting, problem, and so forth. But graphic organizers also make excellent prereading tools for expository text in content-area classrooms. Prior to reading a text, ask students to think about what they already know about a topic. Then ask them to construct a concept map (see Chapter 3) showing what they already know about the topic.

Suppose you're presenting a lesson on muscles. Ask students to first make their own diagram showing what they know about muscles. Perhaps all one student knows is that there are two types of muscles: voluntary and involuntary. This student might show on his diagram that he knows the heart is an involuntary muscle, while a leg muscle is a voluntary one. On the other hand, a student who is very interested in bodybuilding and has extensive background knowledge on the subject might create a more intricate web that shows his knowledge.

Having students compare their graphic organizers and discuss their prior knowledge can help set the stage for the new learning and motivate students. After the lesson, students should compare pre- and postlearning graphs to see how much they have learned about the topic. A good example of a graphic organizer for this strategy is the Compare and Contrast Chart shown in Figure 4.4.

Figure 4.4
Compare and Contrast Chart

Prior to Reading:	
Voluntary Muscles	Involuntary Muscles
After Reading:	
Voluntary Muscles	Involuntary Muscles

Round-Robin Brainstorming

Another fun way to have students brainstorm what they already know on a topic is the Round-Robin technique. Let's say you want to introduce students to the circulatory, skeletal, digestive, excretory, and muscle systems in a unit about the body. Begin by assigning a large sheet of chart paper for each topic (there are five in this case) and lay or hang the charts around the room. Assign students to a group, provide each group with a marker, and ask them to create a concept map on the first chart. After three to five minutes, ask students to move to the next chart. At this chart, students should read the concept map created by the previous group and add any additional information that they can. Students can also place a question mark next to any information that they feel might not be correct. Have the groups repeat the process for every chart. When they return to their original charts, ask the students to read all the information and respond to any question marks that may have been placed by other groups. Post the charts around the room so that additions or corrections can be made as the unit progresses.

Jigsaw Reading

Teachers often complain that students do not read what they are assigned. This is often due either to students being unmotivated or to the difficulty of the text. Most high school textbooks are written at least two grade levels above the average grade level of the students who read them, so it is likely that many students will be unmotivated to struggle through a whole chapter on their own. Many content-area teachers try to solve this problem through round-robin oral reading, but this technique neither builds reading skills nor helps comprehension and retention of content material. The jigsaw technique, however, does both.

Place students in mixed ability groups, with one advanced, two average, and one struggling student in each group. Assign each group a section of the text to study. Ask each group to read the material in whatever manner it wants, whether silently or out loud. Ask the students to take notes as they read and place sticky notes by text that they don't understand. After the reading, have each group discuss the material to ensure that students understand all the concepts presented and that there are no remaining questions. Each group must develop a way to present the information to the rest of the class. Once all groups have prepared their sections, have them make oral presentations, using support materials, in the order in which the materials are presented in the text. Students not presenting should be required to take notes and ask questions of the presenting "experts" until they too understand the material.

Word Association

Give students a list of 8 to 10 new or key words from a text they are going to read. Ask the students to examine the words and create relational graphic organizers showing how they think the words will be related to one another, or how they think the author will fit them in the text. Have the students share their diagrams with the class; after reading the text, examine the diagrams and correct them as needed.

Text Highlighting

Do not assume that your students know how to find the important facts in a given text or properly highlight main points as they read. One way to teach these skills is to find short magazine or newspaper articles in the content area that can be copied on an overhead transparency. Model how you would read the article by reading and thinking aloud about the key details of the passage. Demonstrate how to decide what to highlight in the text by highlighting on the transparency and then sharing your rationale for doing so. After doing this for a few articles, give the students an article and ask them to highlight key ideas themselves. When they are done, ask students to share what they've highlighted and why with partners or a small group. Reinforce highlighting skills by continuing to model and think aloud from time to time for students.

Semantic Feature Analysis

Ask students to create a chart with rows of items and columns labeled with features that the items might share. For example, in a unit on insects, the columns might be labeled as follows: wings, six legs, eight legs, stinger, and hard shell. Each row may be allocated to a different bug: a beetle, a bee, a moth, a ladybug, and a spider. As students discover the attributes of the various insects, have them place a plus or minus in the box corresponding to both the trait and the insect being examined. These charts can also be done on butcher paper so that students can update them over time. See Figure 4.5 for an example of a semantic feature graphic.

Figure 4.5
Semantic Feature Map

Insects	Wings	Six Legs	Eight Legs	Stinger	Hard Shell
Beetle	+	+	-	-	+
Bee	+	+	-	+	-
Moth	+	+	-	-	-
Ladybug	+	+	-	-	+
Spider	-	-	+	-	-

What's My Line?

This activity is a fun way to reinforce student prediction skills and interest students in reading a text. The strategy works for both narrative and expository text. Select approximately 8 to 10 short phrases from the text that convey key ideas and write each one on an index card. Write the same words on four other sets of cards, so that you can divide the class into five groups of three or four students each. Have each group examine its set of cards and think about the relationship that might exist between the words. Without talking to any other groups, each group then writes a paragraph describing what it thinks the text will be about based on the words on the card. Prior to reading the text, the groups should read their paragraphs aloud to the class. After reading the text, have the students determine which group came closest to predicting its actual content.

For variety, a whole-class version of this activity can also be done. Prepare enough phrase cards so that each student can receive his own card. Have the students circulate around the room silently, showing one another their cards until time is called. You will want to allow enough time so that each student can see about one-third to one-half of all the cards in the room. Students are not allowed to make any notes, and must try to remember all the phrases they saw when circulating. When time is called, ask the students to form groups of three or four and try to construct a "gist" paragraph using the key words they remember. The groups then read their paragraphs to the entire class and compare them for accuracy after reading the text. Students will have fun, will love interacting with their peers by being up and moving, and will remember much more of the content.

Learning by Analogy

An excellent strategy for content teachers involves comparing new concepts to ones with which students are already familiar. The parts of an eye, for example, can be compared to the parts of a camera, so that students can understand each function more easily. Assign various concepts to students, and ask them to decide upon an appropriate analogy for the topic. Students enjoy the chance to be creative and can often come up with some interesting and unusual comparisons.

A to Z Brainstorming

Divide the class into groups of two to four students. Ask each group to write the alphabet on a large sheet of chart paper. Tell the groups what topic they will be studying, and ask them to discuss the topic and write either a word or a short phrase beside each letter. The object is to fill in as many letters on the grid as possible that relate to the topic. For example: If the topic is weather, students might write the word "clouds" under C, the word "storm" under S, and so forth, until they have exhausted their ideas. After the groups have had sufficient time to complete at least half of the chart, call time and construct a classroom version of the A to Z chart that includes the answers from all the groups. Students can discuss their words and how they relate to the topic. If you create a large wall chart, it can stay up throughout the lesson so that words can be added under each letter as they are discovered or learned.

Around the World

Identify about five key concepts on the topic to be studied. For example, for a unit on world cultures, you might identify land features, religion, form of government, lifestyle and traditions, and economic information. Put up five numbered sheets of poster paper with a different topic heading on each. Provide the students with markers, and have them count off from one to five. On a signal from you, the students should go to the poster with the number they called and write what they know about the topic in list form until you call time; at that point, they should move on to the next poster, read the listed entries, and try adding facts that the previous group left out. Repeat the process until each student has visited all of the posters in the room, at which point you should gather all the posters and read the entries to the class. The class can add any additional ideas that they come up with. Display the chart in the room until the unit is over; as the unit progresses, add new facts to each chart.

Guess and Check Logs

Guess and Check Logs are good for predicting the content of fictional texts or biographies. Have students bring in small, spiral-bound notebooks and divide the pages into three columns. Ask them to make the first column about an inch wide, and divide the rest of the page into two larger columns. The first column should be labeled "Chapter," the second column "What I Predict Will Happen," and the third column "What Actually Happened." Ask students to write a prediction in their notebooks prior to beginning each chapter. After they have read the chapter, have them go back and recount what actually did happen in the third column of the page. For an example of a Guess and Check Log, see Figure 4.6.

Study Guides

It is helpful for students to know specifically what you think is important as they begin to read a passage. Help them identify

Figure 4.6
Sample Guess and Check Log

Chapter	What I Predict Will Happen	What Actually Happened
1	I think the boy will get the dog he wants.	The boy got a cat instead of the dog he had wanted.

important key points and information by writing a two- to three-page summary of each chapter. Write the summary in chronological order, leaving blanks in the place of key words that you want students to be responsible for learning. As students read the text and find the key terms, have them fill in their study guide appropriately. The study guides should contain much of the information that will appear on the unit test, so that students can know exactly what information you deem important. Students can save the study guides in a loose-leaf notebook for end-of-course tests as well. Figure 4.7 shows an example of a blank study guide.

Figure 4.7
Sample Study Guide

In the past year, the euro has risen more than _____ against the dollar. The rise is because of _____ concerns, like the war in Iraq, rather than economic factors. Over the past five years, the euro zone's real gross domestic product has _____ that of the U.S. by _____. Because it is harder to _____ workers in Europe, European countries do not _____ workers like their U.S. counterparts do. Weinberg believes that the euro is about 10 percent _____.

Word Splash

Put 8 to 15 words or phrases on the blackboard or on a transparency. Ask students to write a prediction paragraph based on the words on the list. Have them put the words together and write a "gist" statement predicting what the text might be about. This exercise increases student interest in reading since the students all want to test their theories and see how close their predictions are to the actual text.

Jots and Doodles

As students silently read a text, have them jot down thoughts or visual representations that occur to them. They might note important information, write down an interesting or unusual sentence, make note of a question, or record an unfamiliar word. After all students have read the material, have them take turns sharing all the "jots and doodles" they've compiled. As each "jot" is read or "doodle" is shown, other students may respond, offer a comment, or help clarify a confusing point or unknown word.

Follow the Leader

Before beginning this exercise, set the purpose and goal for the class. You may ask students to read about how clouds are formed and create a picture to show understanding, for example, or read about key issues behind the Vietnam War and display what they have learned in a graphic.

Students approach reading in different ways. For example, some might prefer reading material silently and then discussing the text with a partner to ensure good understanding; others might prefer taking turns reading out loud before completing a follow-up activity as a group. Divide students into groups of three or four. Appoint one student to lead each group. This student should discuss options with the group and help it decide how to approach the material. The group leader is also responsible for keeping the group on task. Other group members may take on other roles as needed as the work progresses.

Seeing Connections

Students who have difficulty seeing relationships may also have difficulty drawing conclusions, making inferences, and predicting outcomes. One way to develop this skill is to provide students with many opportunities to classify objects. There are many excellent graphic organizers that can be used for this purpose. Classification activities can be simple, such as a diagram of wheels with spokes, or complex, such as a detailed concept map. It is also important for students to discuss why they've grouped items the way they have, and to hear how other students handled the same material.

Patterns

Students can become better readers by understanding the typical patterns that narrative and expository text follow. For example, narrative text usually follows this pattern: establishment of the setting, introduction of the characters, and presentation of the problem or conflict that the lead characters will face. After this, the author usually presents several problems that characters must face as the narrative builds to a high point of dramatic tension. This is usually followed by the characters learning to cope with the problems or overcoming them, followed by a resolution to the story. The entire story, when taken together, establishes a theme or main idea. When students understand the format, they can better identify the key points in the story.

Typical patterns of paragraph development in expository text include the following: examples and illustrations, process outlines, comparisons and contrasting statements, discussion of causes and their effects, definitions, analogies, and analysis. Helping students identify key signal words for different patterns is also helpful. For example, signal words for comparisons and contrasting statements include *similarly, by contrast, same, different, however, but, instead, although, on the other hand, more than, less than, least, most,* and *other.* Graphic organizers that suit each pattern can be helpful as well (see Figure 4.8 for an example). Once students get used to using the organizers, they will be able to spot which type will best help them organize different types of data on their own.

Figure 4.8
Sample Graphic Organizer for Patterns

Butterfly and Moth

Comparisons

Butterfly	Moth
Has wings	Has wings
Can fly	Can fly

Contrasts

Butterfly	Moth
Many colors	Solid color — often brown

Reading Strategies

To build strong reading and thinking skills, students need to engage in as much active reading as possible, both in and out of school (Allington, 2001). Making meaning is what reading is all about; without comprehension, students are simply turning the pages and looking at the words. Some strategies for reading in the classroom appear on the following pages.

Partner Reading

There are two types of partner reading: shared reading, where students share the reading by taking turns reading sections aloud; and silent reading, during which students stop at key points to discuss what they've read. For high school and middle school readers, it is better to allow them to decide which method they wish to use during partner reading. Students choosing shared reading should decide how much of the text each partner will read and how they will alternate. Struggling readers and English-language learners often will prefer the shared reading process, as reading aloud helps them comprehend the material better; more fluent readers, on the other hand, may choose to read silently because it's quicker. Teachers should assign the reading pairs for students through the 6th grade, but older students can be allowed to choose their own partners.

Thinking Aloud

Though the "thinking aloud" strategy has been around since the mid-1970s, Davey (1983) was the first to suggest that students would benefit from hearing how fluent readers think while reading to make meaning from a text. According to Davey, taking a "peek" into a fluent reader's thought process helps struggling readers learn how to think about print, monitor their own comprehension, and apply self-correcting strategies as needed when reading.

The strategy is simple: fluent readers verbalize their thoughts while reading, and less fluent readers listen. Once students learn the technique, ask them to try it themselves. Be sure to provide support and redirection during the process. If you have an especially demanding content area, such as mathematics or science, model thinking aloud for the whole class so that everyone can understand how they should approach the new material.

My Translation Paragraphs

Some struggling readers don't understand that good readers often reread texts for clearer understanding. After reading a text, ask students to break into pairs or small groups to write "my translation" paragraphs in a group log to summarize sections of the text. You can look over the "translations" to spot any misunderstandings or areas where further clarification might be needed. A good way for language arts teachers to help students see the effects of rereading is to read poetry and compare how their levels of understanding change as they reread the poem and discuss the content with others.

Stopping Points

While students read silently, provide them with sticky notes to insert into the text whenever they find a confusing point or want to ask a question about what they are reading. In narrative texts, students can place the notes wherever they have an observation to make, find a link to something in their own background, or come across an interesting sentence or comment. At a signal from you, have all readers stop and turn to a partner or small group and discuss each other's notes.

Text Patterns

Teach students to identify the organizational patterns that they find in content text: sequence orders, lists, descriptions, comparison and contrast statements, cause-and-effect observations, and problem-and-solution constructions. You should also help students identify signal words. Some examples include the following:

- For descriptions: *for example, the characteristics are, includes, such as, also, for instance.*

- For sequence orders: *first, second, finally, next, before, after, then, later, now, on.*

■ For comparison and contrast statements: *similarly, by contrast, same, different, however, but, instead, although, on the other hand, more than, less than, least, most, other.*

■ For cause-and-effect observations: *if, then, thus.*

Note-Taking Strategies

Have students divide the pages in their notebooks into two columns: one labeled, "What I Already Know About . . ." and another labeled "What I Just Learned About . . ." As the students read, have them add to both sides of the notebook. Another option is to label the first column, "Notes from the Book" and the second column, "Notes and Questions from Me."

Who Can Summarize?

Read a section of text to students, ensuring that there are no breaks in continuity or fluency. At key points, stop and ask, "Who can summarize what we have just heard?" Allow time for the students to reflect and provide a summary of the key information that has been presented. As students provide the information, jot some notes on the key points on the chalkboard. Ask students to copy the information into their notebooks. For expository text, you have now provided students with a summary of the data you want them to learn; for narrative text, students now have a deeper understanding of the story.

Echo Reading and Choral Reading

Getting students to model good fluency and reading expression is especially helpful for classes with a high number of struggling readers or English-language learners. In echo reading, students attempt to read a passage exactly as you have modeled it for them. In choral reading, groups of students take turns reading sections in unison without hearing you model it first. (A short poem or Reader's Theater text works best for this strategy.) Choral reading is especially useful for older elementary readers who still need to improve their fluency. For struggling readers, echo reading is particularly effective in one-on-one tutoring sessions with a fluent tutor.

Visualizing the Text

Effective readers know how to visualize the text as they are reading; they can "see" the characters, the setting, and how the action unfolds. Many struggling readers, on the other hand, say that they cannot visualize the text even when teachers tell them to "pretend to see a movie" in their heads.

Teachers can help students develop this skill using the "think aloud" strategy. Find short passages or picture books that have a lot of description. As you read, stop the narration periodically to discuss how the images described in the text appear in your mind. Ask other students to add details of their own. Sometimes students are better able to "see" the pictures being painted by the author if they close their eyes. As you continue reading, stop again and ask students to describe how their pictures might have changed. Asking students to stop and draw what they are thinking about instead of describing it can also be helpful.

Another strategy to increase visualization skills is to ask questions such as: "What do you think the character looks like in this scene?" "If we were making a movie of this passage, what might we want to put in the scene?" "Who can re-create the action in her mind and describe what just happened for us?" It can also be helpful to have students respond to the statements, "When I read this I thought about . . ." and "I could picture . . ."

Taped Readings

Taped readings are the perfect approach for language arts teachers who need to help struggling readers improve both fluency and comprehension skills. Make an audio recording in a moderately slow and expressive voice of a passage that the students have selected. Have students listen via headsets to the tape several times, following along with the printed text. As the readers become more practiced, they read along, trying to emulate as much as possible the speakers' expression and flow. When the students feel that they can read the passage on their own, have them read to a fluent adult reader, who in turn provides feedback on what the reader has done well. The students should continue to practice reading the text until they can do so smoothly and with good expression without the tape. When this passage is mastered, provide the students with a new one that they have selected. (See Chapter 2 for additional information on taped reading.)

Books on Tape

Struggling readers may be able to listen to books that they might never get through otherwise. While listening to books on tape does not take the place of actual reading time, it can provide benefits, such as increased vocabulary and background knowledge. For best results, find contemporary audio books that match the readers' interests.

Sticky-Note Reading

Give students three to five sticky notes of various colors. As the students read, ask them to locate specific elements of the story, such as setting, conflict, or resolution, and mark each with a note. You can also ask students to mark areas that provide specific information, such as the personality of the main character. After the reading, ask students to compare their selections; have them settle any disagreements by referring to the page and sentence indicated on their sticky notes. When reading expository texts, students can be encouraged to mark sections of the text that they found hard to understand. They can also use the sticky notes to locate important facts in nonfiction text.

Concept-Details Notes

In the concept-details note-taking method (Feathers, 1993), students write the names of concepts on the left side of a page and supporting key details on the right side. These notes can then easily be studied for tests. See Figure 4.9 for an example.

Figure 4.9
Sample Concept-Details Notes for the Great Lakes

Concepts	Key Details
Lakes	• Individual lakes: Superior, Michigan, Huron, Ontario, and Erie
Largest freshwater system on earth	• Visible from space
	• 94,000 square miles
	• 1/5 of world's water supply
	• 6 quadrillion gallons of water
	• 10,000 miles of coastline
Many people live around the Great Lakes	• 1/10 of U.S. population
	• 1/4 of Canadian population

After-Reading Strategies

After they've read a text, we want students to be able to summarize, evaluate, and draw their own conclusions about the material. Ideally, they will be able to draw comparisons between texts they have read (text-to-text connections), between the text and themselves (text-to-self connections), and between the text and their knowledge of the world (text-to-world connections). Below are some after-reading strategies that language arts and content-area teachers can use to strengthen student understanding.

Teach a Lesson

Have groups of three to four students present a lesson to their peers on any information that they learned from their reading. Students in the audience should be responsible for taking notes and asking clarifying questions when needed. The groups can choose new words that they find interesting to present to their peers. Each group should explain to the teacher why the information presented is important.

Cloze to Assess Basic Comprehension

To assess a student's skills in using context clues and illustrations, give students a passage with strategically placed blank spaces in key sentences. Ask the student to tell you what word she predicts could fill in the blanks, and to explain how this conclusion was reached. If the student picks an appropriate word based on context cues, such as the rest of the words in the sentence or in-text illustrations, then she does not need to further develop this skill.

Draw the Text

Have students make drawings to illustrate what they learned from the text. After reading a narrative text, they can draw their favorite character or favorite scene. After reading an expository text, students can draw the relationships they learned, portray an important understanding, illustrate a sequence of events, construct a diagram, or make a representation of an important concept in the text.

Note Card Facts

Before reading, give small groups of students 8 to 10 note cards per group. As students read, they are to locate key facts or concepts from the text and write one on each card. After the reading, collect the cards and process the information with the class as a whole. Similar facts should be grouped together and recorded on the board. The class should suggest ways to convey the facts and concepts as clearly, completely, and concisely as possible. Then have students return to the text material and discuss whether any important points were left off the list on the board.

Just the Facts

As students read, ask them to either summarize the key details of the text into a three-minute newscast or to write a news article summarizing the five Ws. Remind students that in a television newscast time is precious, so they should stick to only the main ideas in their presentation. News articles should be clear and easily read, and should provide all of the pertinent details. They should be written as though the information is breaking news—an article on penicillin, for instance, might discuss a "recent discovery" in medicine. Information on key historical figures or events might even be presented as human-interest stories.

Act It Out

Have students mark their favorite scene in a book with a sticky note. Ask them to explain why they have selected the scene, and to construct a script to act it out. The students then perform the scene to demonstrate their understanding. Also acceptable: presenting a speech or soliloquy written from a specific character's perspective.

Write About It

There are many ways for students to write about a text to show comprehension. They can write about a similar experience, rewrite the text from a different perspective, create a different ending or a sequel, turn the text into a play or poem, or write about a favorite part or character from the story.

Retelling Key Events

When students are first learning to retell key events or information, you might want to provide a framework for them to use to organize their thoughts. Here are examples of frameworks for use with text:

Narrative Text Framework

■ The story takes place in

_____ .

■ The main character(s) is (are)

_____ .

■ A problem happens when

_____ .

■ The problem is solved when

_____ .

■ The story ends when

_____ .

Expository Text Framework

■ The main idea of the passage is

_____ .

■ The first main point of the article is

_____ .

■ The second main point of the article is

_____ .

■ The third main point of the article is

_____ .

■ The point the author is trying to make is

_____ .

Always teach students how to summarize narrative text before moving on to expository text, since students find expository text more complex and demanding.

Somebody Wanted—But-So

In the "Somebody Wanted—But-So" technique developed by Macon, Bewell, and Vogt (1991), students learn to summarize the action of a story, historical event, or scientific occurrence by identifying key elements. First, the students identify the "somebody"—that is, the protagonist of the story. They then decide what the person tried to do and what problem prevented him from doing so—the "but." Lastly, the students describe how the person solved the problem—the "so." For an example of a "Somebody Wanted—But-So" document, see Figure 4.10.

Figure 4.10
Sample "Somebody Wanted—But-So" Document

Somebody Wanted	But	So
Cinderella wanted to go to the ball.	But she didn't have anything to wear.	So her fairy godmother appeared and gave her clothes.
The fairy godmother wanted Cinderella to be home by midnight.	But Cinderella was having fun and lost track of time.	The fancy clothes that the fairy godmother had given to her turned back to rags, and she had to run away from the ball.
The handsome prince was in love with Cinderella and wanted to marry her.	But he didn't know where to find her.	So he took the glass slipper that he had found and tried it on every girl in the kingdom until he found the girl whose foot it fit.

Two-Column Journals

There are many ways to have students keep two-column journals as they read. One example is to have them complete quote-and-reflection journals. In the first column, ask students to insert a quote from the text. In the adjacent column, have them write their own thoughts about what the quote might mean.

Another option is to have students label the first column as "Notes from the Book" and the second column "Notes from My Mind." Be sure to regularly provide students with time to share their thoughts and their journal contents with classmates.

It Says, I Say

Drawing inferences is a difficult skill for students to learn. In this two-column journal strategy, students visualize the connection between what they are reading and what the text is actually saying; it's particularly useful with difficult text or poetry. Students should copy the literal passage from the text into the first column, and their interpretation of the text in the second column. Students can use their charts to help one another make sense of the passage or poem after reading (see Figure 4.11).

Figure 4.11
It Says, I Say

It Says	I Say	And So
What the text says	What I think the text means	How do I interpret this?
"Just start to sing when you tackle the thing that 'cannot be done,' and you'll do it." By Edgar A. Guest. From the poem, "It Couldn't Be Done" (Russell, 1984).	Keep a positive attitude when things are difficult and you can succeed.	It is helpful to remember that attitude is very important when things become difficult. If I keep a positive attitude when life is difficult, I will be able to do more than if I tell myself that the task is too hard to accomplish.

Memories

Ask students to write three things that they remember about the topic being studied. When they're done, collect the papers and compile a list of class "memories," making sure to correct any inaccuracies as you go. Another idea is to tell students to write everything they know about the topic within a specific time frame. Collecting the quick write-ups will help you assess what students have gained from the unit, as well as identify any misunderstandings they may have.

Wall Mural

Help students recall a sequence of events by creating a wall mural of key scenes in chronological order. Obtain a long piece of butcher paper and attach it to the classroom wall. Divide the mural into a specific number of scenes, and the class into the same number of groups, assigning each group to a scene. Ask students to review their assigned sections and draw pictures that they think would best illustrate the scene. Have them sketch the drawings on scratch paper before transferring them, with greater detail, to the butcher-paper mural. Students will enjoy adding scenes to the mural throughout the year.

Cinquains

Help students think about the material they are learning by creating short content poems in a cinquain format. For a three-line cinquain, use the following criteria:

- Line 1: A word that is the topic. Example: *Worms.*

- Line 2: Two or three words that describe the topic. Example: *Wiggly, squirmy.*

- Line 3: One or two words that give a feeling about the topic, or a word that is a synonym for the topic. Example: *Nightcrawler.*

For a five-line cinquain, the criteria are as follows:

- Line 1: A noun that is the topic of the poem. Example: *River.*

- Line 2: Two adjectives that describe the topic. Example: *Wet, cool.*

- Line 3: Three words that end in *-ing.* Example: *Rushing, whispering, babbling.*

- Line 4: A phrase related to the topic. Example: *Journeying to the ocean.*

- Line 5: A synonym for the topic. Example: *Old Man River.*

Making Connections

Students should write about or discuss connections between the text and their background knowledge. You can provide starter phrases. For narrative text, use phrases such as: "This reminded me of . . . ," "My favorite part was . . . ," and "Something similar that happened to me was . . ." For expository text, try phrases such as: "When I thought about [detail], this finally made sense to me," "At first, I thought . . . but now I think . . . " "This reminded me of . . ."

Many additional strategies for creating fun, inviting after-reading activities can also be found in Chapter 5. You will want to use a variety of activities to maintain student interest.

Conclusion

Wise teachers who want to strengthen their students' literacy skills know that intermediate and adolescent students thrive on active involvement and love socially stimulating activities. They like to "do" rather than "receive" learning. The students who come through our classroom doors today are used to a high-energy lifestyle. Capitalize on this in your classroom by planning strong before-, during-, and after-reading activities that engage them in learning and motivate them to be involved. Peers are important to students in these age ranges, and they enjoy the interaction of partner and small-group work. Get students up and moving around and interacting with one another, and the interest level and vitality in your classroom will soar.

Help students verbalize their understandings and misunderstandings. Teach them the skills to actively monitor their own comprehension, and support them by using strategies such as activating background knowledge, using graphic organizers and reading guides, and making predictions prior to and during reading. Model thinking aloud for students often, and ask them to explain their own thinking on a regular basis. Remind them often that reading *is* understanding, and that it is up to each of them to practice, question, and learn new techniques to improve their literacy development. After all, only with well-developed literacy and thinking skills will they become capable of meeting the demands they will face in the high-tech economy of tomorrow.

Higher-Order Thinking

The ultimate goal of literacy instruction is for students to be able to process text at the level of evaluation, synthesis, analysis, and interpretation. This level is the final thread in the reading tapestry. Once students have learned to read, we spend most of our time from 3rd grade on trying to help them develop their thinking skills and use them as tools to process their thoughts. As Alvermann and Phelps (1998) tell us, "The curriculum must expand to include information and activities that explicitly support students in learning to think well. The emphasis is less on the mastery of information measured by a recall-based assessment and more on learning how to use one's mind well, to synthesize and analyze skillfully" (p. 69). Put plainly, students will need these higher-order skills to succeed in their lives and careers.

Readers who engage in higher-order thinking go beyond the basic levels of comprehension outlined in Chapter 4. They can analyze, synthesize, evaluate, and interpret the text they are reading at complex levels. They can process text at deep levels, make judgments, and detect shades of meaning. They can make critical interpretations and demonstrate high levels of insight and sophistication in their thinking. They are able to make inferences, draw

147

relevant and insightful conclusions, use their knowledge in new situations, and relate their thinking to other situations and to their own background knowledge. These students fare well on standardized tests and are considered to be advanced. They will indeed be prepared to function as outstanding workers and contributors in a fast-paced workplace where the emphasis is on using information rather than just knowing facts.

Bloom's Taxonomy and Beyond

Although most teachers learned about Bloom's Taxonomy (Bloom, 1956) during their preparation courses, many seldom challenge students beyond the first two levels of cognition: knowledge and comprehension. Because most jobs in the 21st century will require employees to use the four highest levels of thinking—application, analysis, synthesis, and evaluation—this is unacceptable in today's instructional programs. We must expect students to operate routinely at the higher levels of thinking.

Bloom's original taxonomy has certainly withstood the test of time, but a newer version has been introduced to reflect more contemporary thinking. Recently a former student of Bloom, Lorin Anderson, and a group of cognitive psychologists published a revised version of Bloom's taxonomy (Anderson & Krathwohl, 2001). Bloom's original six categories were nouns: knowledge, comprehension, application, analysis, synthesis, and evaluation. In the new version, Anderson and colleagues changed the nouns to verbs to reflect thinking as an active process.

Revised Category #1: Knowledge → Remember

In the revised taxonomy, the original "Knowledge" category was changed to "Remember." This category refers to shallow processing: the drawing out of factual answers, recall, and recognition. In reading, this is simply recalling the facts in a text or recalling the sequence of a story. At this level, questions that teachers ask center on the five Ws and seldom require students to advance beyond superficial thinking. We see this level of thinking often reflected in classrooms across the United States. Some verbs that teachers use to demonstrate student knowledge of material include the following: *choose, describe, define, identify, label, list, locate, match, memorize, name, omit, recite, recognize, select,* and *state.*

Revised Category #2: Comprehension → Understand

The second category of Bloom's original taxonomy was "Comprehension." In the revised model, it is renamed "Understand." This category reflects the acts of translating, interpreting, and extrapolating. Examples in reading include summarizing text and identifying in-text relationships. Some verbs that teachers use to ask students to demonstrate understanding include the following: *classify, defend, demonstrate, distinguish, explain, express, extend, give an example, illustrate, indicate, interrelate, infer, judge, match, paraphrase, represent, restate, rewrite, select, show, summarize, tell,* and *translate.*

Revised Category #3: Application → Apply

The third category, "Application," was changed to "Apply" in the revised taxonomy and is defined as knowing when or why to apply certain skills automatically, as well as having the ability to recognize patterns that can transfer to new or unfamiliar situations. Teachers prompt students to think at the "Apply" level by using the following constructions: "Predict what would happen if . . . ," "Judge the effects of . . . ," and "What would happen if . . . ?" Verbs that teachers might use to determine whether students are working at this level include the following: *apply, choose, dramatize, explain, generalize, judge, organize, paint, prepare, produce, select, show, sketch, solve,* and *use.* When students have not processed information at the application level, they cannot take information learned in one context and translate it to another.

Revised Category #4: Analysis → Analyzing

The "Analysis" category in Bloom's taxonomy was renamed "Analyzing" in the revised version. This level involves breaking information down into parts and different forms, and drawing comparisons between a text and background knowledge data. Classroom questions that address this category include the following: "What is the function of . . . ?" "What conclusions can we draw from . . . ?" "What is the premise?" and "What inference can you make about . . . ?" The following verbs apply to analyzing activities: *analyze, categorize, classify, differentiate, distinguish, identify, infer, point out, select, subdivide,* and *survey*. To use the thinking process of analyzing, students must be able to see connections and draw conclusions. We often see questions on state reading proficiency tests that expect students to display thinking at this level.

Revised Category #5: Evaluation → Design

Though Bloom placed "Evaluation" at the highest level of his taxonomy, Anderson and colleagues rank it fifth to reflect their idea that creative thinking (design) is more complex than critical thinking (evaluation). For the Anderson theorists, critical thinking is necessary for the creative process to occur, because it involves accepting or rejecting ideas—a precursor to creating a new design (Anderson & Krathwohl, 2001). For this reason, evaluation precedes creation in the revised model.

To evaluate information, students need to be able to distinguish essential data from information that is simply interesting. They must be able to identify core themes, form and support opinions, and identify inconsistencies, bias, or lack of coherence or accuracy in a text. They must also be able to use background information, prior knowledge, and other textual sources to assess the validity of the text. For example, when reading a novel, students with strong evaluation skills might compare the works of two authors and offer evidence to support opinions on the author's writing style. Constructions that address the evaluation level include the following: "Do you agree with . . .?" "What is your opinion of . . . ?" "How would you prove. . . ?" "How would you rate . . . ?" and "How would you prioritize . . . ?" The following verbs apply to evaluation activities: *appraise, assess, check, compare, conclude, criticize, critique, defend, justify,* and *support.*

Revised Category #6: Synthesis → Create

The fifth level of the original Bloom's Taxonomy was called "Synthesis." In Anderson's revised version, this level is renamed "Create" and is upgraded to level six. Synthesizing text involves linking new information with prior knowledge or with multiple texts to develop a new idea, establish a new way of thinking, or create a new product of some type. An example of synthesis would be rewriting "Little Red Riding Hood" from the perspective of the wolf. Anderson sees the act of "creating" as combining elements into a pattern that had not existed before. Some constructions that assess the process of analysis or creating include the following: "Develop a new way to . . . ," "Suggest another way to . . . ," "How might you adapt . . . ?" and "Can you predict the outcome if . . . ?" The following verbs signal the "Create" level of thinking: *choose, combine, compose, construct, create, design, develop, formulate, hypothesize, invent, make, make up, originate, organize, plan, produce,* and *role play.* To succeed at this level, students must be able to synthesize their thinking and make predictions based on knowledge.

Focusing Attention on the Higher Levels of Reading

When readers interpret text, they are providing their own ideas about what the content means by applying background knowledge to analyze and synthesize the information. Good readers must interpret both the literal and the implied meaning behind an author's words. The less background knowledge they have on a topic, the more they need to infer meaning by "reading between the lines." Keene and Zimmermann (1997) identified the following seven essential comprehension strategies that skilled readers need to know:

- Determining importance
- Relating the new to the known
- Synthesizing
- Inferring
- Asking questions
- Creating sensory images
- Monitoring for meaning

Each of these topics must be taught to students in a deliberate and direct fashion. When students have mastered all seven strategies, they are processing text at the highest levels of literacy. For their part, Moore and colleagues (2003) point to the following reading skills as particularly important:

- Connecting knowledge to prior experiences
- Previewing and predicting to improve comprehension
- Organizing information and applying meaningful frameworks and categories
- Being able to see, hear, feel, smell, or taste what is described in print
- Self-monitoring of understanding
- Critically evaluating text
- Forming judgments
- Applying the knowledge gained from the text to new situations

Content instruction should strive for depth rather than breadth. To process what they read with insight and a critical eye, students must be able to consider the text as a whole and understand what the author is trying to communicate. Students may demonstrate understanding by explaining the purpose or viewpoint of a text, identifying the theme and critical elements, sharing their opinions on some aspect of the story, or analyzing the personal attributes of a character and interpreting his actions. Students must also be able to create and understand analogies, write about their thoughts and opinions, compare and contrast similar or dissimilar events, and use their creativity to extend and develop concepts. Higher-order thinking skills will allow them to analyze pros and cons and form well-reasoned opinions as adults.

In addition to good technical reading skills, students must have a good grasp of the nuances of language and how words are used. Figurative language can be particularly difficult for students. Petrosky (1980) observes that adults on average use figurative expressions over 500,000 times during a year; they permeate our texts as well as our speech patterns, helping to clarify meaning. Figurative language requires readers to access background knowledge and relate concepts to one another. According to Readence, Baldwin, and Head (1986), there are three reasons that readers may have difficulty interpreting figurative language: they may not recognize that the language is not meant literally, or they may not have enough background knowledge to understand the link between the two compared items. English-language learners are particularly stymied by figurative language, and by idioms in particular. Acting out idioms or illustrating them literally are fun ways to help the class interpret them. Have students construct their own picture books of favorite figurative phrases. Poems are great sources of rich figurative language, as are newspapers and magazines—especially the ads. Ask students to bring some examples to class. Some fun books for learning about figurative language are *In a Pickle and Other Funny Idioms* (1983) by Marvin Terban and *Chocolate Moose for Dinner* (1976) and *The King Who Rained* (1970), both by Fred Gwynne.

At the time this book went to press, the following Web sites were available to help increase student vocabulary and comprehension:

- The Wacky World of Words Web site (http:// www3.bc.sympatico.ca/teachwell/), where teachers can get games, puzzles, and other fun activities for all types of word and phrase learning.
- The RhymeZone (http://www.rhymezone.com/), where students can find rhymes, synonyms, and antonyms for any word they type in, as well as resources on Shakespeare, Mother Goose, and famous quotes and documents.
- Word Play (http://www.wolinskyweb.net/word.htm), an exhaustive list of Web sites devoted to words of all kinds. I guarantee that your students will love exploring many of the sites listed; take time to explore them yourself and see how fascinating and helpful they can be.

Doing Well on High-Stakes Tests

As a result of state mandates and the No Child Left Behind act, teachers everywhere are concerned about helping their students do well on state and national assessments. If we want students to succeed, we must understand one important fact: Students can only do well on these tests when they are accustomed to providing on a regular basis the types of responses that the tests demand. Ask them to identify the most important ideas in a chapter, to prepare summaries, and to think deeply about how the information can be synthesized, analyzed, evaluated, and interpreted.

We cannot and should not try to "prep" students for specific tests. Instead, we must teach them how to think. One technique that all teachers can use is the "Talk Through" strategy developed by Simpson (1995), in which students are asked to individually share their thinking about a text. For example, you might say to students, "Talk through the key ideas of the passage" or "Talk through the passage's examples and details to help us find the key ideas." To take the discussion to higher levels, ask students to talk through their personal connections and experiences with the key ideas, or to talk through their reactions to the key ideas presented. Engaging students in this manner will force them to go beyond the simple-knowledge level of thinking.

Beck, McKeown, Hamilton, and Kucan (1997) suggest a strategy called "Questioning the Author." In many high-stakes tests, understanding the writer's craft is a requirement for students to do well. "Questioning the Author" involves asking students what they think the author is trying to say. Ask students questions such as "Did the author explain this clearly?" and "Does this make sense given what the author told us before?"

On state writing tests, students will often be expected to write an expository or persuasive passage, or to analyze a narrative passage. To help your students do well on these tests, demonstrate how to understand what the instructions require by thinking aloud. Consistently assist students in analyzing instructions thoroughly before they begin to write. Most states provide examples of the kinds of reading and writing tasks students will face. Be sure to get copies of these samples and study them carefully so you know what will be expected of the students.

On many standardized tests, students are expected to analyze a narrative text by examining the writer's style and the way the story and the characters are developed, interpreting various aspects of the text, and identifying the story's themes. Students will need to be able to see relationships and patterns and draw conclusions about the characters' motives and behaviors. They must demonstrate that they have a thorough grasp of the meaning of the text. At the elementary level, students should be able to identify the theme of a story, any morals that might be suggested, and elements of character, setting, plot, problem, and resolution. Older students should be able to discuss the theme as well as any symbolism in the story, and to offer their analysis, evaluation, and opinions of the text. An excellent source for good writing-prompt ideas and examples of well-organized narrative, persuasive, and expository texts can be found at the Northwest Regional Lab's Six Traits Web site (http://www.nwrel.org/assessment/department.php?d=1).

To perform well on essay questions regarding expository text, students should use a consistent tone and focus their thoughts. Organization is assessed according to the strength of the introduction, the thesis and supporting details, and the conclusion. Show students good examples of texts that conform to these criteria. Students should also understand how to vary sentence types and patterns, use descriptive vocabulary to express their ideas, and have a clear sense of audience as they write. Content-area teachers can assist their language arts peers by frequently having students write and explore expository passages in their discipline.

Students may also be asked to write persuasive essays on state or national tests. To do well on these essays, students must understand how to support a position with evidence and factual details, anticipate alternative viewpoints, and provide thoughtful arguments to counter those viewpoints. Again, texts should include strong introductory and concluding statements.

The National Assessment of Educational Progress Standards

You have probably heard of the National Assessment of Education Progress (NAEP) test, but do you really know what it is and how it is used? The test is a national reading exam authorized by Congress and administered by the U.S. Department of Education to randomly selected segments of 4th, 8th, and 12th grade students in the United States (National Center for Educational Statistics, 2003). Its purpose is to provide a snapshot of educational progress levels across the nation in various subject areas. The test examines three contexts for reading: reading for literary purposes, information, and to perform a task. Because many state tests ask similar types of questions as those used in the NAEP, examining the test's format is particularly helpful to teachers.

Examining the NAEP specifications helps us understand what our students are expected to know and be able to do. You can find a summary of these expectations in Appendix C. As you read through them, consider how you can address these performance indicators daily in your classroom.

Teaching Higher-Order Thinking Skills

Teachers are good at writing and asking literal questions (e.g., "Name the parts of a flower"), but we tend to do this far too often. Students must be taught to find the information they need, judge its worth, and think at higher levels. There is simply too much information in the world for us to waste students' time with regurgitations of basic facts. As Bellanca (1997) states:

> Educators need to realize that there are many more ways to teach than by rote alone. There is teaching for understanding, decision making, problem solving, and connecting a part to a whole, detail to concept, and concept to concept. There also is inference, prediction, analysis for bias, and learning for transfer. Each of these processes requires some form of critical thinking. All are processes that students can develop and refine. Opportunities for students to develop critical thinking processes are not found in classrooms dominated by the regurgitation of short answers. They are found in classrooms where active learning is an essential component. (pp. xxi–xxii).

The old instructional paradigm asked students to read from the textbook and discuss the information to see if they learned the content. We then would test them on the material, lament over how many did poorly, move on to the next topic, and repeat the cycle. When we begin applying what we know about reading and learning, the effective content classroom will look quite different from this model. In the new paradigm, we will

- Design prereading activities to activate background knowledge, establish purpose, and formulate questions that can drive inquiry.
- Allow students to use active reading methods that include peer discussion, as well as to try out their thoughts and seek clarifications from one another as they are reading.
- Model our own thought processes for students and ask that they make their own thinking visible as well.
- Design activities that require students to process information at the highest levels of thought.
- Examine our state curriculum standards to cull out the essential topics so that we can extend learning with greater depth, rather than try to teach curriculum that is a mile wide.

Strategies for Extending Thinking

Below are strategies for content teaching that extend learning to the higher levels of thinking. You can find additional strategies about this in my previous book, *The Threads of Reading: Strategies for Literacy Development* (Tankersley 2003).

Directed Reading and Thinking Activity

The directed reading and thinking activity (DR-TA) developed by Stauffer (1969) is still very helpful for processing text of all types at high levels. In the DR-TA, teachers walk students through setting purpose, making predictions, asking questions, and clarifying points in the text. The approach can be used in all content areas, from science to language arts to math.

The DR-TA begins with the students examining the title of the story or section to be read. From this information, they make predictions and set expectations regarding what the text is about. Next, either the teacher reads the material out loud or students read sections, stopping at designated points. Logical stopping points include subheadings, ends of chapters, or high points of a story. At each stopping point, teachers ask open-ended questions designed to elicit predictions or opinions about the text. The more they read, the more focused the students' predictions and opinions should become. Your role is to help maintain this focus by asking students to describe how elements in the text are connected and to provide evidence for any assertions, acting all the while as a nonjudgmental facilitator rather than a participant. The DR-TA structure forces students to justify their thoughts and link their opinions back to the text. As teachers, we can learn a lot about our students by listening to their ideas, values, background knowledge, and reasoning.

Letters from the Heart

Ask students to write a letter about some facet of a book. The letter can be addressed to the author, a historical figure, or a character in the book, and can be written either from the student's perspective or from that of another character. One of the four higher levels of Bloom's taxonomy—application, analysis, synthesis, or evaluation—should be evident in the letter.

Position Paper

Provide students with several articles on a specific topic that present two sides of an issue. Students should read the articles and take notes on points made by both sides. With a partner, they should then pick a side and write a position paper defending their position with factual evidence. Students can also participate in trials or debates on controversial issues. For a more advanced version of this activity, have students pretend they are senators and cast ballots either for or against a particular position. Tallying the votes also helps students practice math skills during the lesson.

Drawing Inferences

Bring in comic strips or political cartoons that require students to infer what the cartoonist meant. Ask students to work with a partner or small group to identify what inferences they need to make to interpret the point of the cartoon, and what connections they need to draw to do so.

"Dear Author" Letters

Ask students to write "Dear Author" letters based on their thoughts about a particular book or piece of writing. Many Web sites offer valuable information and research on a variety of authors.

"Wish You Were Here" Postcards

After reading, ask students to pretend that they are characters in the book and write "Wish You Were Here" postcards to their friends. This strategy is particularly useful during lessons on historical events.

Comparison-Contrast Questions

Ask students to develop comparison-contrast questions and write them in their graphic organizers. Examples: "How is a glove like your hand?" "How is a dog like a cat, and how are they different?" and "What would happen if circles were squares?"

Script Writing

Select a scene from a story and ask students to develop a script from it for Reader's Theater. Have students rehearse the script and present the performance for an audience.

R.A.F.T.

This strategy, developed by Santa (1988), helps students write with a focused purpose. Students can use any format they want—

diary, letter, editorial, and so on—to answer the following questions from the perspective of a character they've read about:

- R is for writer. Who are you?
- A is for audience. Who will read your work?
- F is for format. What type of writing will you do?
- T is for topic. What will you be writing about?

A student could write as Cinderella, for example, thanking her fairy godmother for allowing her to go to the ball, or as George Washington, writing to his wife about the Revolutionary War.

Quickwrite

This is a good strategy for assessing student knowledge and comprehension on a topic. Ask students to take out a sheet of paper and write for 5–10 minutes, describing what they know about the topic and what they are still confused about or hoping to learn.

Seen the Movie?

Find a novel or historical text that has been made into a movie. Have students watch the movie and read the text, then compare and contrast the two versions. If you are using a historical text, see if the students can find inaccuracies or anachronisms in the film version.

Key Question Charts

Provide students with a controversial question, such as "Should companies be allowed to drill for oil in Alaska Artic National Wildlife Refuge?" Give students "pro" and "con" articles to read about the topic, and have them create a chart that lists the pro argument on one side and the con argument on the other. Ask the students to form an opinion of their own after carefully evaluating the data, and to provide a thorough analysis of their reasoning.

Diaries

Ask students to create a diary of a prominent or historical character related to the event or topic being studied—Thomas Jefferson, say, or a soldier in Vietnam. If more contemporary subjects are used, ask students to interview original sources with firsthand knowledge about the topic, and to compile their memories into a single diary that reflects how people thought and felt at the time of the event. Another form of this activity is to ask students to describe "a day in the life" of someone during the time period being studied, or to write a letter from that same perspective.

Rewriting Stories

Ask students to think of a story that they all know, such as "Little Red Riding Hood" or "Goldilocks," and to list the places, characters, and events that the story features. After rereading the tale, have the students update the list and see what elements they forgot. For a more advanced version of this activity, ask students to read three or four different versions of the same fairy tale and list the ways in which they differ.

Read-Paraphrase

Having students rewrite in their own words what they've read helps them develop deeper levels of comprehension. Ask students to stop reading at regular intervals to do this. Begin by modeling what you want them to do, and then allow them to paraphrase text with partners or in small groups of three or four. Give students no more than three sections to read in a textbook, and ask them to write a summary of the key ideas in 20 words or fewer. As students become comfortable with the process, ask them to make observations or ask questions about the material. Have each group share its summaries as a lead-in to more in-depth study of the topic.

Pro-Con-Interesting Fact

Provide students with a controversial statement or question. Have them work in small groups to make a chart containing three columns labeled "Pro," "Con," and "Interesting Facts." Ask students to research the topic and categorize the information they find under the three categories, form an opinion about the question, and then discuss their findings with the class.

Idea Web

Help students remember what they have learned by creating a wall graphic to represent their knowledge. On wall-sized mural paper, draw a circle in the center and write the name of the topic being studied. You might also write a question in the circle (e.g., "What do you think about the environment?" or "What is communism?"). Place chalk or markers in a basket in front of the mural. Tell students to approach the writing area in an orderly fashion and silently add to the mural by connecting a bubble with their own comments in it to the main bubble. Students may add as many links as they want, and may link to other people's comments as well as to the main bubble. You may participate as well, adding your own thoughts or ideas to the unfolding web. Allow plenty of wait time before deciding that the web is complete; students need time to read the comments and think about what has been added.

In another version of this strategy, pass a piece of paper around the room and have each student write something meaningful about the topic being studied. Have students sign their entries to ensure "seriousness" on their part.

Oxymorons

Have students collect oxymorons—terms that contain inherent contradictions, such as "true lies"—and add them to a classroom mural.

Book Symbols

Ask students to bring in five items that represent the book they have read and present them to the class, describing what they represent and why.

Modeling Children's Books

Many wonderful children's books can be used for patterning a new book. For example, you might ask students to read a book and create their own versions, employing the same patterns as the original. The books can then be presented to younger schoolmates as a holiday gift. This is a great activity for students serving as classroom reading buddies.

Conclusion

Learning to synthesize, evaluate, and process information in new ways is the key to preparing students for the world outside of school. We can no longer leave literacy development to language arts teachers. All teachers must learn to model their thinking processes and "make the invisible visible" to students. With the tightening of the higher-order thinking thread, the literacy weave will be complete.

Conclusion

Reading is the foundational skill that determines whether a student will succeed in school or become just another dropout statistic destined to become society's burden. For far too long, educators have been too complacent, waiting for students to come to learning instead of bringing the learning to them. We cannot wait for primary support systems to provide us with better readers; we must help our struggling middle and secondary students today.

In my first teaching job, I taught two periods of remedial reading in high school. The administrator who hired me saw that I had six credits of reading on my college transcript and decided that I had the knowledge to do the job. I was eager to be hired, so I agreed that I could do the job. When I finally met my new students, I realized that I didn't have a clue how to help them—their reading skills ranged from virtually illiterate to at most a 4th grade level. I later learned that I was just one of 15 English teachers in the 2,700-student high school who were tasked with a period or two of remedial classes. Most of the teachers were new, like me, and had little background in working with high school students with reading problems. Many of my colleagues planned lessons to keep the students busy while making little effort to solve their reading problems.

I was both amazed and appalled by these students. Although I didn't know what to do to help them, I was determined to learn. Fortunately, my mother-in-law, a special education teacher, was able to assist me and gave me valuable suggestions. Although we did make some reading progress that year, I certainly did not know how to make up for the 10 or so years of missed opportunities that some of these students had. In addition to my mother-in-law's advice, I immediately began a master's program in reading at the local university.

As a first-year teacher, I hadn't even figured out how to manage the content area that I had been trained to handle, much less teach a class in which I had no background. I often think about these students and wonder how much more progress they could have made had they had a teacher who was truly skilled in reading instruction instead of a beginner with very little knowledge. Alas, that was not meant to be.

If I could have a "do-over" with those kids, there is so much I would do differently now, with 28 years of teaching wisdom under my belt. First, I would begin my class every day by reading aloud to all of my students for 10–15 minutes, because struggling students need to hear fluent reading being modeled. When reading aloud, I could also model to my students such skills as prediction, making connections, anticipation, and questioning. If I were teaching with an elementary school nearby, I would arrange for my students to be "reading buddies" with younger students and practice reading picture books to them at least once a week. If no elementary children were available, we would simply write ABC books or picture books to give as gifts to a neighboring school.

Because I now know that reading skills build on a foundation of phonemic awareness, I would have any preliterate students in my class study vocabulary by making webs and playing games with new words, learning sight words in phrase form, and working with peers on simple texts at the appropriate level of difficulty. We would examine phoneme groups and spend time learning rime patterns, both in games and from Word Walls. I would make audio recordings of high-interest, low-vocabulary materials that the students deemed interesting. Students would listen to these tapes with headphones, practice reading along with them, and after mastering the material, read it to me for feedback. I would also keep an abundance of commercial audio books in the room and allow students to regularly listen to them.

Our class would track ongoing progress in student reading logs. Every day, students would read poetry and song lyrics chorally or by echoing me, paying special attention to word groupings, inflection, and the rhythm of the language. We would also write our thoughts down together every day, and keep track of the books we were reading. I would teach students different strategies to use when they came across new words or text they did not understand; students would practice these strategies daily with partners, and talk through ways to approach and visualize what the text describes. We would write Reader's Theater scripts about our lives and practice them as a group, ideally tying the text to topics the students are studying in other classes. We would research our favorite movie stars and singers on the Web and prepare reports to present. The class would be alive with activity—reading, talking, and having fun with books and language. Students would be excited to come to class and eager to see what would be happening each day.

For students with strong decoding skills, I would emphasize building fluency, expanding vocabulary, improving comprehension, and developing higher-order thinking skills. I'd ask them to become "word collectors," bringing in new words for the Word Wall. We would study prefixes, suffixes, and root words to help with the decoding of unknown words, and practice tearing words apart to see how they're composed. We'd use picture books as models for books that we would create and give to younger students. We'd begin studying authors we thought were interesting. We would develop our own shows, complete with sound effects and props, and take them on the road to other classes. We'd set a purpose for reading by using graphic organizers to help us focus on meaningful parts of our task. We would read, read, and read—as individuals, pairs, and small groups—practicing silent and oral reading skills thoroughly. We would research authors on the Internet and with library resources and maybe even hold debates on some of our topics. Students would leave the classroom still discussing or arguing about the text and groaning that it was time to move on to their next class.

Unfortunately for the 54 students who passed through my door that first year, my classroom did not look like the one described above. All I knew how to do was read a book with rotating groups of students while others worked quietly and independently on "skill-drill" workbooks. Of course, we cannot have "do-overs," and life has gone on for those 54 students. I apologize to them for not having been trained, at the time, in what I'd been asked to do.

The good thing about teaching is that each year we have the opportunity to expand our learning and improve our instruction. We get to grow into masterful teachers who know exactly how to assist each learner who crosses our thresholds. Over the years, I have trained many teachers to do just what I would like to have done with my first class. I have watched eager students come to classrooms where learning is exciting and stimulating. I have seen them glued to books, deep in discussion, and engrossed in projects that displayed their learning. It is my hope that this book will help you leave a strong literacy legacy to your students. May you become a master weaver in your own classroom.

Appendix A

Sample Reader's Theater Script for Social Studies

Note: This example is based on my experience with students' real-life Reader's Theater scripts. Script-writing is an appropriate technique for all students in grades 4–12. The script contained here was adapted from McGann, T. F. (1971). The ordeal of Cabeza de Vaca. In R. G. Athearn (Ed.), *The American Heritage New Illustrated History of the United States, Vol. 1: The New World* (pp. 83–88). Uncasville, CT: Fawcett Publishers.

"The Ordeal of Cabeza de Vaca"

Narrator: The year was 1528. Forty Spanish sailors, tired and weary, drifted in the ocean. They were all that was left of the great Navaez expedition, which had set out from Spain in June of 1527 with five ships and 600 men to explore the new world.

Sailor 1: Look! The shore at last. Come and let us make our way to the beach!

Narrator: They crawled onto the sandy beach to find food, water, and dry land. On the shore, they finished what little corn they had and drank from rotting water carriers. It was November.

Sailor 2: At least the land stands still and does not rock and toss us about, as we have suffered for weeks on end.

Sailor 1: But it seems our comrades who went ashore to search for the gold we were told about are lost, and we will never see them again.

Sailor 2: I agree, my friend. It was unwise of the Captain to send them ashore. Our supplies are low and little remains of our corn. I fear for our lives as well.

Captain de Vaca: Lope, go scout this area and report back to me at once!

Lope: Aye, Captain. (Lope leaves the beach area.)

Narrator: And so the men rested while Lope searched the area where they had landed.

Lope: Captain, Captain! We seem to be on a small island. There is water all around. See off in the trees, three men with bows and arrows follow and hide in the shadows.

Captain de Vaca: You did well, Lope. Hopefully, we can make friends with the natives. Our provisions are low. Perhaps they can help us to find food and fresh water.

Narrator: The Indian natives brought fresh fish and roots to the starving men. The Spaniards gave them trinkets in return. The Indians took pity on the men and took them to their huts and warmed them.

Sailor 3: Look how the natives dance and howl. Do you think they mean to cook us and eat us?

Sailor 4: My fear continues to grow. I don't know what all of this means. I can only hope they intend to spare our lives.

Sailor 3: Me too.

Narrator: The next day, 50 more Spaniards wandered into camp. This crew had landed a few miles further up the beach. The ranks of Spaniards now neared 90. Winter came and life was hard on the small island. There was little food, and many of the Spaniards and the Indians died.

Sailor 5: This place is bad luck. I will name it "Malhado"—Bad Luck Island.

Sailor 6: Yes, this place must have great bad luck—see how the natives survive even though they wear little or no clothes.

Sailor 5: Did you see how they tried to cure Vasquez by blowing on him with a stick?

Sailor 6: Yes, I laughed at them for that. That is why we will get no food tonight. They said we will not eat until we do as they tell us.

Sailor 5: Well, I for one will continue to say my prayers over Vasquez.

Narrator: In the spring of 1529, only 12 Spaniards remained. One additional man had appeared, so the group of 13 set off for Mexico.

Lope: I am sorry my friends, I cannot go with you. I am too weak to travel. Alaniz and I will remain on Malhado.

All sailors: Goodbye, old friend. We will try to send for you when the weather warms and you are better. De Vaca will also watch over you and keep you safe.

Narrator: Although life was harsh and food was scarce, Cabeza eventually recovered from his illness and set himself up as a trader in the new world. He traveled among the Indian tribes to gather shells, sea beans, and other goods to trade for skins, ocher, and flints. Each year, he would return to Malhado to see Lope.

Captain de Vaca: Lope, you must not remain in this horrible place. Come with me to the mainland and work with me.

Lope: I cannot swim, so how can I cross to the mainland?

Narrator: The Indians treated the sailors badly and life was harsh on the island. In September of 1534, the four remaining Spaniards managed to slip away from their Indian captives. They stayed with a new group of Indians for eight months and learned some skills as medicine men.

Captain de Vaca: We will travel to Mexico to meet our friends, but we must go inland. The inland Indians are kinder than the coastal Indians.

Lope: Perhaps we can find the cities of riches and gold on our journey.

Captain de Vaca: Yes, maybe we will.

Narrator: The four travelers wandered around the countryside laden with gifts and exercising authority over the Indians. They received gifs of flour and corn, roasted quail, and venison in abundance. They crossed the Rio Grande and continued west across the passes of the Sierra Madre, toward the coast.

Sailor 4: Captain, the Indians tell me that they have seen others like us in this area. They say that they come on horseback.

Sailor 3: The Indians call themselves "Christians."

Captain de Vaca: I will ask the Indians to take me to their captain. I will ask him for the year, to certify the day on which we arrived in this new world.

Narrator: And so, the Indians took the small group of Spaniards to the other Spanish explorers. The meeting did not go well, and the group was met with suspicion and hostility. They pushed on to Mexico City where they were greeted by the viceroy, Mendoza, and the explorer and conqueror, Cortez.

Mendoza: Captain de Vaca, you and your men are brave and bring honor to Spain.

Captain de Vaca: Thank you, Viceroy, but I have lived among the Indians for so long that it is difficult to wear clothes upon my body or sleep anywhere but on the ground.

Sailor 1: Yes, I too find it difficult to live among civilized men again.

Sailor 2: We will miss you as you return to Spain, Captain. We have learned well how to live under your guidance these past eight years.

Narrator: De Vaca returned to Spain for a few years, but returned to the Americas in 1540 as governor of Paraguay.

Political difficulties led to his recall and imprisonment. He returned to Spain and remained there until his death in the 1590s. The remaining sailors settled in the new world until their deaths. Alvar Nuñez Cabeza de Vaca's travels paved the way for later explorers such as Marcos de Niza and Francisco Vasquez de Coronado in the great Southwest.

Appendix B

Fluency Rubric

Lowest level of fluency. At this level, students

- Read in a flat monotone with little or no expression.
- Show little evidence of connectivity or phrasing.
- Read haltingly, and may pause at length to study individual words.
- Disregard punctuation.
- Do not pick up on shifts in speaker or author style.
- Exhibit limited comprehension.
- Have trouble relating a sequence of events or textual details.

Second-lowest level of fluency. At this level, students

- Read in a flat monotone.
- May occasionally group two to three words into a meaningful unit but spend more time on decoding than expression.
- Recognize some punctuation, but not consistently.
- Occasionally pick up on shifts in speaker or author style.
- Have limited comprehension, but can recall details and events.

Middle level of fluency. At this level, students

- Read mostly in phrases.
- Exhibit some intonation.
- Occasionally read in a monotone, but add more tonal fluctuations.

- Attempt to recognize shifts in speaker or author style.
- Recognize and follow common punctuation marks such as periods and commas, but may disregard other ones.
- Begin to increase comprehension.
- Can provide key details and sequence events from the text.

Second-highest level of fluency. At this level, students

- Can read mostly in phrases or complete sentences.
- May stumble over decoding, but find that such problems are less frequent.
- Attempt, however inconsistently, to vary pitch, expression, pacing, and tonality when reading aloud.
- Heed all punctuation marks most of the time.
- Exhibit strong comprehension.
- Can provide key details and some smaller details from the text, as well as a correct and fairly detailed sequence of events.

Highest level of fluency. At this level, students

- Employ strong expression and tonality and vary pitch and pacing when reading aloud.
- Observe all punctuation marks.
- Pick up on all shifts in speaker or author style.
- Exhibit very strong comprehension.
- Can provide extensive details and subdetails from the text, as well as a correct and fairly detailed sequence of events.

Appendix C

National Assessment of Educational Progress (NAEP) Expectations

Note: Adapted from the National Center for Education Statistics (2003). *National Assessment of Educational Progress (NAEP) Reading Assessments.* Washington, DC: Institute of Educational Sciences, U.S. Department of Education.

4th Grade Expectations

The NAEP standards for 4th grade students specify that they should know how to

- Demonstrate overall understanding of the text by providing inferential as well as literal details and interpreting the text.
- Identify the author's use of specific details.
- Explain character motivation and identify a story theme.
- Summarize a story.
- Draw conclusions about the characters or plot and recognize relationship patterns such as cause and effect.

To be considered "advanced," students must be able to

- Demonstrate awareness of how authors compose and use literary devices.

■ Judge texts critically and provide insightful analysis.

■ Identify the author's illustration of theme through the story action.

■ Make generalizations about the point of the story and integrate such insights with personal experiences and background knowledge.

■ Identify figurative language.

■ Compare story characters and their changing feelings.

■ Interpret story action.

■ Provide alternative endings.

■ Describe character traits and lessons learned by characters in the text.

■ Compare story characters using metaphors.

■ Explain the author's intent with supporting material.

■ Contrast historical information with present-day information.

■ Make critical judgments about the text and be able to clearly explain and communicate ideas.

■ Use ideas gained from the text to elaborate on hypothetical situations.

8th Grade Expectations

At the 8th grade level, the NAEP prescribes that proficient students should be able to

■ Show overall understanding of both literal and inferential material in the text.

■ Extend ideas and draw clear inferences.

■ Summarize text.

■ Draw conclusions from and make personal connections to the text.

■ Provide examples (both implied and explicit) to support literary themes and interpret the actions and motives of characters.

- Recognize literary devices such as personification and foreshadowing.

To be considered advanced, students should be able to

- Describe abstract themes and overall ideas in the text by analyzing both meaning and form.
- Support conclusions with examples and extend them through comparisons to personal experiences and world events.
- Provide complex summaries of text.
- Describe various literary elements such as setting, plot, characters, and theme, and discuss how they interact with one another.
- Analyze the author's style and evaluate the composition of the text.
- Identify the main idea in informational text, and the author's purpose in writing it.
- Make inferences and draw conclusions supported by details in the text.
- Determine the relationships among facts, ideas, and events.
- Understand the concepts of cause and effect and time-order.
- Identify a central purpose and predict the outcomes of procedures specified in informational text.

12th Grade Expectations

To meet proficient status, 12th grade students must be able to

- Demonstrate an overall understanding of both inferential and literal information.
- Extend text ideas by making inferences, drawing conclusions, and connecting the text to personal experiences or background knowledge.
- Explain literary devices such as irony and symbolism.

■ Apply knowledge learned from informational text to specific situations.

■ Apply steps or directions appropriately and be able to evaluate the usefulness of data in informational text.

To be considered advanced, 12th grade students should be able to

■ Identify abstract themes and overall ideas.

■ Analyze meaning and form, using details from the text to support conclusions.

■ Develop extensive responses that make reference to personal experience and background knowledge.

■ Create complex summaries of the text.

■ Incorporate cultural, historical, and personal information sources to evaluate the text, and to develop and explain conclusions and perspectives.

■ Identify the relationship between the author's point of view and elements of the text, and analyze and evaluate that point of view.

■ Advance new responses to problems or issues and apply knowledge from informational texts to new situations.

■ Critically evaluate the usefulness of informational text and apply directions to new situations.

Bibliography

Ackerman, P. T., & Dykman, R. A. (1996). The speed factor and learning disabilities: The toll of slowness in adolescents. *Dyslexia, 2,* 1–21.

Adams, M. J. (1990). *Beginning to read: Thinking and learning about print.* Cambridge, MA: The MIT Press.

Allen, J. (1999). *Words, words, words: Teaching vocabulary in grades 4–12.* York, ME: Stenhouse Publishers.

Allington, R. L. (1977). If they don't read much, how are they ever gonna get good? *Journal of Reading, 21,* 57–61.

Allington, R. L. (1980). Poor readers don't get to read much in reading groups. *Language Arts, 57,* 872–877.

Allington, R. L. (2001). *What really matters for struggling readers.* New York: Addison-Wesley.

Allington, R. L. (2002). You can't learn much from books you can't read. *Educational Leadership, 60*(3), 16–19.

Alvermann, D. E., & Phelps, S. F. (1998). *Content reading and literacy: Succeeding in today's diverse classrooms.* Boston: Allyn and Bacon.

Anderson, L., & Krathwohl, D. A. (2001). *Taxonomy for learning, teaching, and assessing: A revision of Bloom's taxonomy of educational objectives.* New York: Longman.

Anderson, R. C., & Nagy, W. E. (1991). Word meanings. In R. Barr, M. Kamil, P. Mosenthal, G. P. D. Pearson (Eds.), *Handbook of Reading Research, Vol. 2* (pp. 690–724). New York: Longman.

Anderson, R. C., & Nagy, W. E. (1992). The vocabulary conundrum. *American Educator, 16*(4), 4–18, 44–47.

Armbruster, B. B., Lehr, F., & Osborn, J. (2001). *Put reading first: The research building blocks for teaching children to read, K–3.* Washington, DC: The Partnership for Reading.

August, D., & Hakuta, K. (1997). *Improving society for language-minority children: A research agenda.* Washington, DC: National Academies Press.

Avi. (1990). *Something upstairs.* New York: William Morrow.

Baker, S. K., Simmons, D. C., & Kameenui, E. J. (1995). *Vocabulary acquisition: Synthesis of the research.* (Tech. Rep. No. 13). Eugene, OR: National Center to Improve the Tools of Educators, University of Oregon.

Baumann, J. F., & Kameenui, E. J. (1991). Research on vocabulary instruction: Ode to Voltaire. In J. Flood, J. J. D. Lapp, & J. R. Squire (Eds.), *Handbook of research on teaching the English-language arts* (pp. 789–814). New York: Longman.

Beck, I. L., & McKeown, M. G. (1983). Learning words well: A program to enhance vocabulary and comprehension. *The Reading Teacher, 36,* 622–625.

Beck, I. L., & McKeown, M. G. (1998). Comprehension: The sine qua non of reading. In S. Patton & M. Holmes (Eds.), *The keys to literacy* (pp. 28–36). Washington, DC: Council for Basic Education.

Beck, I. L., McKeown, M. G., Hamilton, R. L., & Kucan, L. (1997). *Questioning the author: An approach for enhancing student engagement with text.* Newark, DE: International Reading Association.

Beck, I. L., McKeown, M. G., & Kucan, L. (2002). *Bringing words to life: Robust vocabulary instruction.* New York: The Guilford Press.

Beck, I. L., Perfetti, C. A., & McKeown, M. G. (1982). Effects of long-term vocabulary instruction on lexical access and reading comprehension. *Journal of Educational Psychology, 74*(4), 506–521.

Beers, K. (2003). *When kids can't read what teachers can do.* Portsmouth, NH: Heinemann Publishers.

Bellanca, J. (1997). *Active learning handbook.* Arlington Heights, IL: IRI Skylight Training and Publishing.

Bereiter, C., & Scardamalia, M. (1987). An attainable version of high literacy: Approaches to teaching higher-order skills in reading and writing. *Curriculum Inquiry, 17*(1), 10–30.

Berninger, V. W. (2002). Revealing the secrets of the brain: Neuropsychologist Virginia Berninger studies brain images before and after instruction for clues to the mystery of learning disabilities [online]. Available: http://www.nwrel.org/nwedu/08-03/brain-t.asp

Berrueta-Clement, J. R., Schweinhart, L. J., Barnett, W. S., Epstein, A. S., & Weikart, D. P. (1984). *Changed lives: The effects of the Perry Preschool program on youths through age 19.* Ypsilanti, MI: The High/Scope Press.

Blachowicz, C., & Fisher, P. (2000). *Teaching vocabulary in all classrooms* (2nd ed.). Upper Saddle River, NJ: Merrill Prentice Hall.

Blachowicz, C., Fisher, P., Costa, M., & Pozzi, M. (1993). *Researching vocabulary learning in middle school cooperative reading groups: A teacher-researcher collaboration.* Paper presented at the 10th Great Lakes Regional Reading Conference, Chicago.

Bloom, B. (1956). *Taxonomy of educational objectives, handbook 1: Cognitive domain.* New York: David McKay.

Bradley, L., & Bryant, P. (1983). Categorizing sounds and learning to read: A causal connection. *Nature, 301,* 419–21.

Brown, M. W. (1990). *The important book.* Hong Kong: Harper Trophy.

Brown, R., & Cazden, C. (1965). *Environmental assistance to the child's acquisition of grammar.* Cambridge, MA: Harvard University. (ERIC Document Reproduction Service No. ED 003 466)

Butts, E. (2004). *Idioms for aliens: A grammar revue of plays and verse.* Gainseville, FL: Maupin House Publishing, Inc.

Campbell, F. A., Pungello, E. P., Miller-Johnson, S., Burchinal, M., & Ramey, C. T. (2001). The development of cognitive and academic abilities: Growth curves from an early childhood educational experiment. *Developmental Psychology, 37,* 231–242.

Carter, R. (1998). *Mapping the mind.* Los Angeles: University of California Press.

Caulkins, L. M. (2001). *The art of teaching reading.* New York: Addison-Wesley.

Chall, J. S. (1987). Reading and early childhood education: The critical issues. *Principal, 66*(5), 6–9.

Chall, J. S. (1996). *Stages of reading development, 2nd edition.* Fort Worth, TX: Harcourt-Brace.

Chall, J. S., Jacobs, V. A., & Baldwin, L. E. (1990). *The reading crisis: Why poor children fall behind.* Cambridge, MA: Harvard University Press.

Chrisp, P. (2000). *Welcome to the Globe: The story of Shakespeare's theatre.* New York: DK Publishing, Inc.

Collins, J. (1986). Differential instruction in reading groups. In J. Cook-Gumperez (Ed.), *The social construction of literacy* (pp. 117–137). New York: Cambridge University Press.

Cope, J. (1997). Beyond voices of readers: Students on school's effect on reading. *English Journal, 86*(3), 18–23.

Cummins, J. (1994). The acquisition of English as a second language. In K. Spangenber-Urbschat & R. Pritchard (Eds.), *Kids come in all languages: Reading instruction for ESL students* (pp. 36–62). Newark, DE: International Reading Association.

Cunningham, A. E., & Stanovich, K. E. (1997). Early reading acquisition and its relation to reading experience and ability 10 years later. *Developmental Psychology, 33,* 934–945.

Cunningham, A. E., & Stanovich, K. E. (1998). What reading does to the mind. *American Educator, 22*(1), 8–15.

Cunningham, P. M. (2000). *Phonics they use* (3rd ed.). New York: Longman.

Cunningham, P. M., Hall, D. P., & Gambrell, L. B. (2002). *Self-selected reading the Four Blocks way.* Gainsboro, NC: Carson Dellarosa.

Cuyler, M. (1991). *That's good! That's bad!* New York: Holt and Company, Inc.

Daggett, W. R. (2004). *Achieving written proficiency for all* [Unpublished white paper]. Rexford, NY: International Center for Leadership in Education.

Davey, B. (1983). Think-aloud: Modeling the cognitive processes of reading comprehension. *Journal of Reading, 27*(1), 44–47.

Dixon, M. B., Wegener, A., & Petruska, K. C. (2001). *Thirty ten-minute plays for two actors.* Manchester, NH: Smith and Kraus, Inc.

Dowhower, S. L. (1987). Effects of repeated reading on second-grade transitional readers' fluency and comprehension. *Reading Research Quarterly, 22,* 389–406.

Durkin, D. (1993). *Teaching them to read* (6th ed.). Boston: Allyn and Bacon.

Eisner, E. (1998). *The kind of schools we need: Personal essays.* Portsmouth, NH: Heinemann.

Eldredge, J. L., Reutzel, D. R., & Holingsworth, P. M. (1996). Comparing the effectiveness of two oral reading practices: Round-robin reading and the shared book experience. *Journal of Literacy Research, 28*(2), 201–205.

Feathers, K. M. (1993). *Infotext: Reading and learning.* Toronto: Pippin.

Fleischman, P. (1985). *I am phoenix: Poems for two voices.* New York: Harper Collins.

Fleischman, P. (1988). *Joyful noise: Poems for two voices.* New York: Harper Collins.

Francis, D. J., Shaywitz, S. E., Steubing, K. K., Shaywitz, B. A., & Fletcher, J. M. (1996). Developmental lag versus deficit models of reading disability: A longitudinal, individual growth curves analysis. *Journal of Educational Psychology, 88*(1), 3–17.

Francis, D. J., Shaywitz, S. E., Stuebing, K. K., Shaywitz, B. A., & Fletcher, J. M. (1997). Early intervention for children with reading disabilities: Study designs and preliminary findings. *Learning Disabilities: A Multi-Disciplinary Journal, 8,* 63–71.

Frayer, D. A., Frederick, W. C., & Klausmeier, H. G. (1969). *A science for testing the level of concept mastery.* Madison: University of Wisconsin Research and Development Center for Cognitive Learning.

Fredericks, A. D., & Stoner, A. A. (2000). *Silly salamanders and other slightly stupid stuff for Reader's Theater.* Portsmouth, NH: Libraries Unlimited.

Fry, E. B. (1980). The new instant word list. *The Reading Teacher, 34,* 284–290.

Fry, E. B., Kress, J., & Fountoukidis, D. L. (1993). *The reading teacher's book of lists* (3rd ed.). Englewood Cliffs, NJ: Prentice Hall.

Fuchs, L. S., Fuchs, D., Hosp, M. K., & Jenkins, J. R. (2001). Oral reading fluency as an indicator of reading competence: A theoretical, empirical, and historical analysis. *Scientific Studies of Reading, 5*(3), 239–256.

Garcia, G. E., Jimenez, R. T., & Pearson, P. D. (1998). Metacognition, childhood bilingualism, and reading. In D. J. Hacker, J. Dunlosky, & A. C. Graesser (Eds.), *Metacognition in theory and practice* (pp. 193–219). Mahwah, NJ: Erlbaum.

Gillet, J. W., & Temple, C. A. (1996). *Language and literacy: A lively approach.* Glenview, IL: Harper Collins College Publishers.

Good R. H., III, Simmons, D. C., & Smith, S. B. (1998). Effective academic intervention in the United States: Evaluating and enhancing the acquisition of early reading skills. *School Psychology Review, 27*(1), 45–56.

Graves, M. F., Brunetti, G. J., & Slater, W. H. (1982). The reading vocabularies of primary grade children of varying geographic and social backgrounds. In J. A. Niles & L. A. Harris (Eds.), *New inquiries in reading research and instruction* (pp. 99–104). Rochester, NY: National Reading Conference.

Gray, S. W., Ramsey, B. K., & Klaus, R. A. (1982). The early training project: 1962–1980. In Consortium for Longitudinal Studies (Ed.), *As the twig is bent: Lasting effects of preschool programs* (pp. 33–69). Hillsdale, NJ: Lawrence Erlbaum Associates.

Grossen, B. (1997). *Thirty years of research: What we know about how children learn to read.* Santa Cruz, CA: The Center for the Future of Teaching and Learning.

Guest, E. A. (1984). It couldn't be done. In W. F. Russell (Ed.), *Classics to read aloud to your children* (p. 225). New York: Crown Publishers, Inc.

Gustafson, C. (2003). *Acting cool! Using Reader's Theater to teach language arts in your classroom.* Worthington, OH: Linworth.

Gwynne, F. (1970). *The king who rained.* New York: Simon and Schuster.

Gwynne, F. (1976). *Chocolate moose for dinner.* New York: Simon and Schuster.

Haggard, M. R. (1982). The vocabulary self-selection strategy: An active approach to word learning. *Journal of Reading, 26,* 203–207.

Hakuta, K., & Snow, C. (1986). *The role of research in policy decisions about bilingual education.* Report to the Committee on Education and Labor, Washington, D.C.

Hart, B., & Risley, T. R. (1995). *Meaningful differences in everyday experiences of young American children.* Baltimore, MD: Brookes Publishing.

Hart, B., & Risley, T. R. (2003, Spring). The early catastrophe: The 30 million word gap by age 3. *American Educator.*

Harvey, S., & Goudvis A. (2000). *Strategies that work: Teaching comprehension to enhance understanding.* York, ME: Stenhouse Publishers.

Heath, S. B. (1983). *Ways with words: Language, life, and work in communities and classrooms.* Cambridge, England: Cambridge University Press.

Heber, H. L., & Nelson, J. B. (1986). Questioning is not the answer. In E. K. Dishner, T. W. Bean, J. E. Readence, & D. W. Moore (Eds.), *Reading in the content areas: Improving classroom instruction* (2nd ed., pp. 210–215). Dubuque, IA: Kendall/Hunt.

Herman, P. A., Anderson, R. C., Pearson, P. D., & Nagy, W. E. (1987). Incidental acquisition of word meanings from expositions with varied text features. *Reading Research Quarterly, 23,* 263–284.

Hirsch, E. D., Jr. (2003, Spring). Reading comprehension requires knowledge of words and the world. *American Educator,* 10–29.

Hobbs, W. (1997). *Bearstone.* New York: Simon and Schuster.

Hutchins, P. (1986). *The doorbell rang.* Hong Kong: Harper Trophy.

Ivey, G., & Broaddus, K. (2001). Just plain reading: A survey of what makes students want to read in middle school classrooms. *Reading Research Quarterly, 36,* 350–371.

Jiminez, R. J. (1997). The strategic reading abilities and potential of five low-literacy Latino readers in middle school. *Reading Research Quarterly, 32,* 224–243.

Johns, J. L., & Lenski, S. D. (2001). *Improving reading strategies and resources.* Dubuque, IA: Kendall/Hunt.

Juel, C. (1988). Learning to read and write: A longitudinal study of 54 children from 1st through 4th grade. *Journal of Educational Psychology, 80,* 437–447.

Kameenui, E. J. (1996). *Learning to read/reading to learn: Helping children with learning disabilities to succeed.* Eugene, OR: National Center to Improve the Tools of Educators.

Keene, E., & Zimmermann, S. (1997). *Mosaic of thought: Teaching comprehension in a reader's workshop.* Portsmouth, NH: Heinemann.

Kismaric, C., & Heiferman, M. (1996). *Growing up with Dick and Jane.* New York: Harper Collins Publishers, Inc.

Kos, R. (1991). Persistence or reading disabilities: The voices of four middle school students. *American Educational Research Journal, 28*(4), 875–895.

Koskinen, P. S., & Blum, I. H. (1999). Shared reading, books, and audiotapes: Supporting diverse students in school and at home. *The Reading Teacher, 52,* 430–444.

Krashen, S. D. (1993). *Every person a reader.* Culver City, CA: Language Education Associates.

Kucera, H., & Francis, W. N. (1967). *Computational analysis of present day American English.* Providence, RI: Brown University Press.

Lane, E., & Shengold, N. (1997). *Take ten: New 10-minute plays.* New York: David McKay.

Langer, J. A. (1999). *Beating the odds: Teaching middle and high school students to read and write well.* Albany, NY: National Research Center on English Learning and Achievement, University of Albany.

Lenz, B. K., & Hughes, C. A. (1990). A word identification strategy for adolescents with learning disabilities. *Journal of Learning Disabilities, 23*(3), 149–158, 163.

Lyon, G. R. (1995). Toward a definition of dyslexia. *Annals of Dyslexia, 45,* 3–27.

Lyon, G. R. (2001, March 8). *Measuring success: Using assessments and accountability to raise student achievement.* Statement for the Subcommittee on Education Reform, Committee on Education and the Workforce, U.S. House of Representatives, Washington D.C. Retrieved February 20, 2003, from http://www.plato.com/pdf/teleconfrence_session3_lyon1.pdf

Lyon, G. R., Shaywitz, S. E., & Shaywitz, B. A. (2003). A definition of dyslexia. *Annals of Dyslexia, 53,* 1–14.

Macon, J., Bewell, D., & Vogt, M. (1991). *Responses to literature: Grades K–8.* Newark, DE: International Reading Association. (ERIC Document Reproduction Service No. ED 325 852)

Marzano, R. J., Pickering, D. J., & Pollock, J. E. (2001). *Classroom instruction that works.* Alexandria, VA: Association of Supervision and Curriculum Development.

McGann, T. F. (1971). The ordeal of Cabeza de Vaca. In R. G. Athearn (Ed.), *The American Heritage New Illustrated History of the United States, Vol. 1: The New World* (pp. 83–88). Uncasville, CT: Fawcett Publishers.

McKeown, M. G. (1993). Creating effective definitions for young word learners. *Reading Research Quarterly, 28,* 16–31.

McKeown, M. G., Beck, I. L., Omanson, R. C., & Pople, M. T. (1985). Some effects of the nature and frequency of vocabulary instruction on the knowledge of use of words. *Reading Research Quarterly, 20*(5), 522–535.

Meltzer, J., Cook Smith, N., & Clark, H. (2001). *Adolescent literary resources: Linking the research and practice.* Providence, RI: Brown University.

Miller, G. A., & Gildea, P. M. (1985). *How to misread a dictionary.* Pisa, Italy: International Association for Applied Linguistics.

Mikulecky, L. J. (1990). Stopping summer learning loss among at-risk youth. *Journal of Reading, 33*(7), 516–521.

Moats, L. C. (2001, March). When older students can't read. *Educational Leadership,* 36–40.

Moore, D. S., Moore, P., Cunningham, P., & Cunningham, J. (2003). *Developing readers and writers in the content areas K–12.* Boston: Allyn and Bacon.

Moore, D. W., Bean, T. W., Birdyshaw, D., & Rycik, J. A. (1999). *Adolescent literacy: A position statement for the Commission on Adolescent Literacy of the International Reading Association.* Newark, DE: International Reading Association.

Moore, D. W., Readence, J. E., & Rickelman, R. J. (1989). *Pre-reading activities for content area reading and learning* (2nd ed.). Newark, DE: International Reading Association.

Nagy, W. E. (1987). Learning word meanings from context during normal reading. *American Educational Research Journal, 24*(2), 237–270.

Nagy, W. E. (1988). *Teaching vocabulary to improve reading comprehension.* Newark, DE: International Reading Association.

Nagy, W. E., & Anderson, R. C. (1984). How many words are there in printed school English? *Reading Research Quarterly, 19,* 304–330.

Nagy, W. E., Anderson, R. C., & Herman, P. A. (1987). Learning word meanings from context during normal reading. *American Educational Research Journal, 24,* 237–270.

Nagy, W. E., Herman, P. A., & Anderson, R. C. (1985). Learning words from context. *Reading Research Quarterly, 20,* 233–253.

Nagy, W. E., & Scott, J. A. (2000). Vocabulary processes. In M. L. Kamil, P. B. Mosenthal, P. D. Pearson, & R. Barr (Eds.), *Handbook of Reading Research* (Vol. 2, pp. 269–284). Mahway, NJ: Earlbaum.

National Center for Education Statistics. (1998). *National Assessment of Educational Progress (NAEP) Reading Assessments.* Washington, DC: Institute of Educational Sciences, U.S. Department of Education.

National Center for Education Statistics. (2001). *National Assessment of Educational Progress (NAEP) Reading Assessments.* Washington, DC: Institute of Educational Sciences, U.S. Department of Education.

National Center for Education Statistics. (2002). *National Assessment of Educational Progress (NAEP) Reading Assessments.* Washington, DC: Institute of Educational Sciences, U.S. Department of Education.

National Center for Education Statistics. (2003). *National Assessment of Educational Progress (NAEP) Reading Assessments.* Washington, DC: Institute of Educational Sciences, U.S. Department of Education.

National Reading Panel. (2000). *Teaching children to read: An evidence-based assessment of the scientific research literature on reading and its implications for reading instruction.* Washington, DC: National Institute of Child Health and Human Development.

National Research Council Committee on Developing a Research Agenda on the Education of Limited English-Proficient and Bilingual Students. (1997). *Improving schooling for language-minority children: A research agenda.* Washington, DC: National Academy Press.

Nord, C. W., Lennon, J., Liu, B., & Chandler, K. (1999). *Home literacy activities and signs of children's emerging literacy: 1993 and 1999.* Washington, DC: U.S. Department of Education.

Ogle, D. (1986). K-W-L: A teaching model that develops active reading of expository text. *The Reading Teacher, 39,* 564–570.

Organization for Economic Cooperation and Development. (2000). *Knowledge and skills for life: First results from PISA 2000* (Table 2.1a). Paris: Author.

Pearson, P. D., Dole, J. A., Duffy, G. G., & Roehler, L. R. (1992). Developing expertise in reading comprehension. In A. Farstup & J. Samuels (Eds.), *What research has to say about reading instruction* (2nd ed.). Newark, DE: International Reading Association.

Pearson, P. D., Hansen, J., & Gordon, C. (1979). The effect of background knowledge on young children's comprehension of explicit and implicit information. *Journal of Reading Behavior, 11,* 201–219.

Petrosky, A. R. (1980). The inferences we make: Children and literature. *Language Arts, 57,* 149–156.

Pinnell, G. S., Pikulski, J. J., Wixson, K. K., Campbell, J. R., Gough, P. B., & Beatty, A. S. (1995). *Listening to children read aloud.* Washington, DC: Office of Educational Research and Improvement, U.S. Department of Education.

Postlethwaite, T. N., & Ross, K. N. (1992). *Effective schools in reading: Implications for policy planner.* The Hague: International Association for the Evaluation of Educational Achievement.

Preston, R. (2002). *The demon in the freezer.* New York: Random House.

Raphael, T. E. (1984). Teaching learners about sources of information for answering comprehension questions. *Journal of Reading, 28,* 303–311.

Rasinski, T. V. (1990). *The effects of cued phrase boundaries in texts.* Bloomington, IN: ERIC Clearinghouse on Reading and Communication Skills. (ERIC Document Reproduction Service No. ED 313 689)

Rasinski, T. V. (2003). *The fluent reader: Oral reading strategies for building word recognition, fluency, and comprehension.* New York: Scholastic.

Rasinski, T. V., Padak, N., Linek, W., & Sturtevant, E. (1994). The effects of fluency development instruction on urban second grade readers. *Journal of Educational Research, 87,* 158–164.

Readence, J. E., Baldwin, R. S., & Head, M. H. (1986). Direct instruction in processing metaphors. *Journal of Reading Behavior, 18,* 325–339.

Readence, J. E., Bean, T. W., & Baldwin, R. S. (1989). *Content area reading: An integrated approach.* Dubuque, IA: Kendall/Hunt.

Restak, R. (2001). *The secret life of the brain.* Washington, DC: Joseph Henry Press.

Ruddell, M. R. (2001). *Teaching content reading and writing* (3rd ed.). New York: John Wiley and Sons.

Samuels, S. J. (1979). The method of repeated readings. *The Reading Teacher, 32,* 403–408.

Samuels, S. J. (1994). Toward a theory of automatic information processing in reading revisited. In R. B. Ruddell, M. R. Ruddell, & H. Singer (Eds.), *Theoretical models and processes of reading* (4th ed., pp. 816–837). Newark, DE: International Reading Association.

Santa, C. (1988). *Content reading including study systems.* Dubuque, IA: Kendall/Hunt.

Scarborough, H. S. (1984). Continuity between childhood dyslexia and adult reading. *British Journal of Psychology, 75,* 329–348.

Schreiber, P. A. (1980). On the acquisition of reading fluency. *Journal of Reading Behavior, 12,* 177–186.

Schreiber, P. A. (1991). Understanding prosody's role in reading acquisition. *Theory into Practice, 30,* 158–164.

Scieszka, J. (1989). *The true story of the three little pigs!* New York: Penguin Group.

Scieszka, J., & Smith, L. (1992). *The stinky cheese man and other fairly stupid tales.* New York: Penguin Group.

Scott, J. A., & Nagy, W. E. (1989, December). *Fourth graders' knowledge of definitions and how they work.* Paper presented at the annual meeting of the National Reading Conference, Austin, Texas.

Searls, E. F., & Klesius, J. P. (1984). Ninety-nine multiple meaning words for primary students and ways to teach them. *Reading Psychology, 5,* 55–63.

Serafini, F. (2001). *The reading workshop: Creating space for readers.* Portsmouth, NH: Heinemann.

Shaywitz, B. A., Fletcher, Holahan, J. M., & Shaywitz, S. E. (1992). Discrepancy compared to low achievement definitions of reading disability: Result from the Connecticut longitudinal study. *Journal of Learning Disabilities, 25*(10), 639–648.

Shaywitz, B. A., Shaywitz, S., Blachman, B., Pugh, K., Fullbright, R., Skudlarski, P., Mencl, E., Constable, T., Holahan, J., Marchione, K., Fletcher, J., Lyon, R., & Gore, J. (2003, June). *Development of left occipito-temporal systems for skilled reading following a phonologically-based intervention in children.* Paper presented at the Organization for Human Brain Mapping, New York City.

Shaywitz, S. (2003). *Overcoming dyslexia.* New York: Alfred A. Knopf.

Shaywitz, S. E., & Shaywitz, B. A. (2004). Reading disability and the brain. *Educational Leadership, 51*(6), 7–11.

Shepard, A. (1993). S*tories on stage: Scripts for Reader's Theater.* New York: H. W. Wilson Company.

Shepard, A. (2003). *Folktales on stage: Sixteen scripts for Reader's Theater from folk and fairy tales of the world.* Redondo Beach, CA: Shepard Publications.

Simpson, M. (1995). Talk-throughs: A strategy for encouraging active learning across the content area. *Journal of Adolescent and Adult Literacy, 38*(4), 296–304.

Smith, J., & Elley, W. (1997). *How children learn to read.* Katonah, NY: Richard C. Owen.

Snow, C. E. (1991). *Unfulfilled expectations: Home and school influences on literacy.* Cambridge, MA: Harvard University Press.

Snow, C. E. (2002). *Reading for understanding: Toward an R&D program in reading comprehension.* Santa Monica, CA: Rand Corporation. Available: http://www.rand.org/multi/achievementforall/reading.

Snow, C. E., Barnes, W., Chandler, J., Goodman, I., & Hemphill, L. (1992). *Unfulfilled expectations: Home and school influences on literacy.* Cambridge, MA: Harvard University Press.

Snow, C. E., Burns, S. M., & Griffin, P. (Eds.) (1998). *Preventing reading difficulties in young children.* Washington, DC: National Academy of Education.

Sousa, D. (1995). *How the brain learns.* Reston, VA: National Association of Secondary School Principals.

Stahl, S. A. (1999). *Vocabulary development.* Cambridge, MA: Brookline Books.

Stahl, S. A. (2003, Spring). Words are learned incrementally over multiple exposures. *American Educator.*

Stahl, S. A., & Fairbanks, M. M. (1986). The effects of vocabulary instruction: A model-based meta-analysis. *Review of Educational Research, 56*(1), 72–110.

Stahl, S. A., & Vancil, S. (1986). Discussion is what makes semantic maps work in vocabulary instruction. *Reading Teacher, 40,* 62–69.

Stanovich, K. E. (1986). Matthew effects in reading: Some consequences of individual differences in the acquisition of literacy. *Reading Research Quarterly, 21,* 360–407.

Stauffer, R. G. (1969). *Directed reading maturity as a cognitive process.* New York: Harper and Row.

Taba, H. (1967). *Teacher's handbook for elementary social studies.* Reading, MA: Addison-Wesley.

Tankersley, K. (2003). *The threads of reading: Strategies for literacy development.* Alexandria, VA: Association for Supervision and Curriculum Development.

Tanner, L. (2004, April 27). Dyslexia may be more common in boys. *The Mercury News.*

Taylor, M. (1999). *The road to Memphis.* Upper Saddle River, NJ: Prentice Hall.

Terban, M. (1983). *In a pickle and other funny idioms.* New York: Houghton Mifflin.

Terban, M. (1987). *Mad as a wet hen.* Boston: Clarion.

Torgesen, J. K., & Burgess, S. R. (1998). Consistency of reading-related phonological processes throughout early childhood: Evidence from longitudinal-correlational and instructional studies. In J. Tetsala & L. Ehri (Eds.), *Word recognition in beginning reading* (pp. 161–188). Hillsdale, NJ: Earlbaum.

Vogt, M. E. (1989). *The congruence between preservice teachers' and inservice teachers' attitudes and practices toward high and low achievers.* Unpublished doctoral dissertation, University of California, Berkeley.

Vogt, M. E. (2000). Content learning for students needing modifications: An issue of access. In M. McLaughlin & M. E. Vogt (Eds.), *Creativity and innovation in content area teaching* (pp. 329–351). Norwood, MA: Christopher-Gordon.

Voss, J. F., Vesonder, G. T., & Spilich, G. J. (1980). Text generation and recall by high-knowledge and low-knowledge individuals. *Journal of Verbal Learning and Verbal Behavior, 19,* 651–667.

Vygotsky, L. S. (1934/1978). *Mind in society: The development of higher psychological processes.* (M. Cole, V. John-Steiner, S. Schribner, & E. Souberman, (Eds. and Trans.). Cambridge, MA: Harvard University Press. (Original work published 1934)

Wallace, J. (1995). Improving the reading of poor achieving students. *Reading Improvement, 32*(2), 102–104.

Weiner, B. (1979). A theory of motivation for some classroom experiences. *Journal of Educational Psychology, 71,* 3–25.

White, T. G., Graves, M. F., & Slater, W. H. (1990). Growth of reading vocabulary in diverse elementary schools: Decoding and word meaning. *Journal of Educational Psychology, 82*(2), 281–290.

Wigfield, A., & Asher, S. (1984). Social and motivational influences on reading. In R. Barr, M. L. Kamil, P. D. Mosenthal, & P. B. Pearson (Eds.), *Handbook of reading research, vol. 1* (pp. 423–452). New York: Longman.

Wolfe, P., & Nevills, P. (2004). *Building the reading brain, PreK–3.* Thousand Oaks, CA: Corwin Press.

Wood, K. (1984). Probable passages: A writing strategy. *The Reading Teacher, 37,* 496–499.

Wylie, R. E., & Durrell, D. D. (1970). Teaching vowels through phonograms. *Elementary English, 47*(6), 787–791.

Yarosz, D. J., & Barnett, W. S. (2001). Who reads to young children? Identifying predictors of family and reading activities. *Reading Psychology, 22,* 67–81.

Index

Note: Entries followed by an *f* indicate figures and tables.

About the Author

Karen Tankersley recently left the public school system after five years as assistant superintendent for Educational Services in a rapidly growing Phoenix-area school district. She now provides staff development and consultation to school districts around the world. Originally a linguist with a B.A. in French and a minor in German and English, she has an extensive background in language and language acquisition issues. Karen also holds an M.A. in reading and a Ph.D. in educational leadership and policy studies from Arizona State University.

In her early career, Karen spent 10 years as a foreign-language teacher, reading specialist, and teacher of the gifted and talented. She served for 12 years as a principal in at-risk schools recognized nationally for their outstanding achievement and high academic performance, has taught at the university level, and has published articles in several educational journals (including *Educational Leadership*). Karen is also the author of *Threads of Reading: Strategies for Literacy Development* (ASCD, 2003). Contact information is available at her Web site: http://www.threadsofreading.com.

www.ingramcontent.com/pod-product-compliance
Lightning Source LLC
Chambersburg PA
CBHW051904090426

42811CB00003B/450